Science GCSE

Bob McDuell, David Baylis and Graham Booth

What this book contains

How to do Rapid Revision

The aim of *Rapid Revision* is simple. It's to help you do better in your exams in a very short time. This book is for active revision – it puts you in charge. In order to do well in your exams you need to:

- have a plan of what you need to know – that's the Action plan on page 4
- quickly target what you need to learn – that's in the Revision units which are at the heart of this book
- be able to learn quickly and effectively
- understand what the examiners are looking for – that's in the grade-boosting tips in the answers.

A few other things you need to know

What exam are you doing for GCSE science?

You may be studying for your GCSE science exam at one of two levels or tiers. Higher tier is intended for students aiming at A*, A, B, C and D grades. (An E grade is awarded for candidates just missing grade D. Below that students are ungraded.) Foundation tier is for students aiming at Grade C, D, E, F and G. About 45% of the questions appear in both tiers. They make up the easier questions on the higher tier and the harder questions on the foundation tier. All science exams in England and Wales are based on the same content. Some exam boards offer module science exams with multiple test questions throughout the course, but the content is the same.

The exam you are studying for will be either Double Award or Single Award science. Double Award means that the exams count as two GCSE subjects.

What does this book cover?

This book covers both Single and Double Award science up to higher tier and all types of syllabus in England and Wales. It will enable you to improve your level of working right up to A* but it will also enable you to turn a Grade D to a Grade C on the higher or foundation tiers.

Don't forget to look at the secrets of success in science on page 6!

How to get going

Step 1

Look at the action plan on page 4. Check on what you need to know. You can start with the first item on the list or you can target something that worries you.

Step 2

Choose a revision unit. The revision units are in three parts:

1 The Check Up

How well do you know the topic? Do this quick check to find out. If it seems OK you can skip the crash course and go straight to the exam practice - or you can go straight on to another unit. Rapid revision means targeting what you need to learn. It's very easy to spend time on things you already know!

2 The Crash Course

That's the bit which teaches you the key facts and skills you must know to do well in the exam. It puts the essential facts and knowledge very clearly and simply - and it's broken into small chunks for easy learning.

3 Exam Practice

These provide GCSE-type questions section by section. They are a real test of what you need to know in the exam. Answers to all the questions come with grade-boosting examiners' tips.

The revision units are really flexible - if you want, just do the crash courses to get the facts - or focus on exam practice close to the exams.

Step 3

Record your progress on the action plan if you want. Then go on to the next unit.

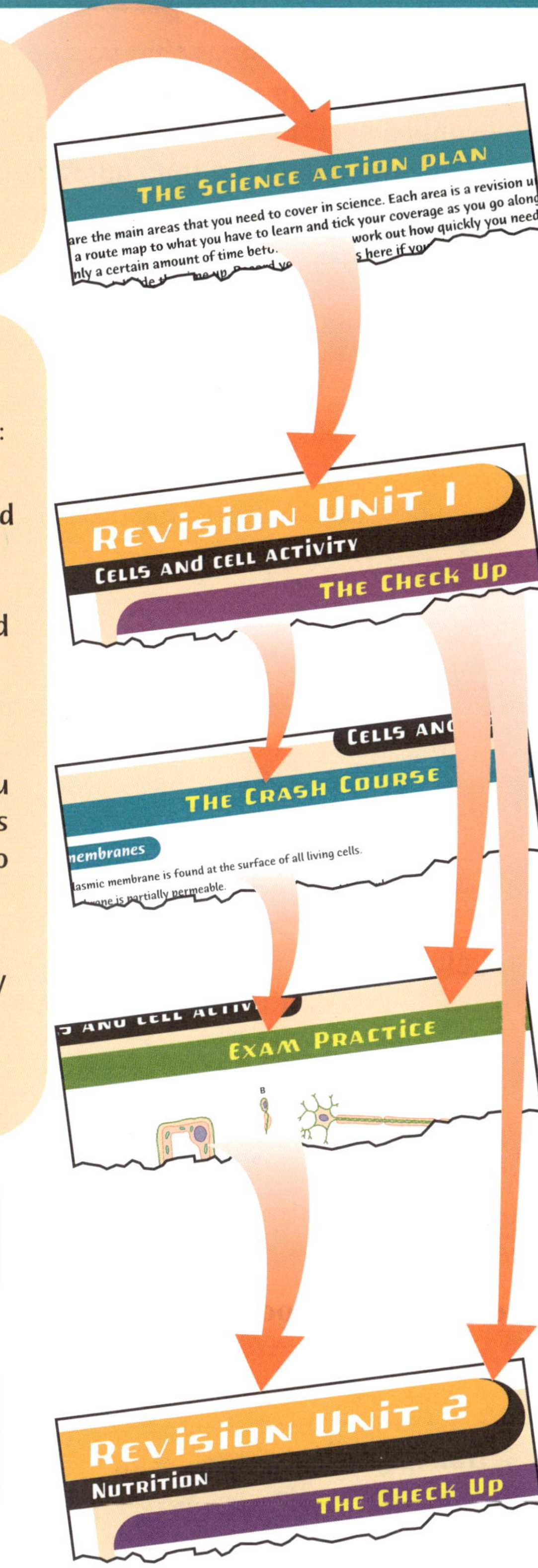

And if you're really short of time …

1 Don't panic.
2 Do The Check ups. Start with the topics you're less confident about. If you do OK, go straight to the next unit. If not, do The Crash Course.
3 Write the key things from The Crash Course you want to remember in note form on cards and pin them to your bedroom wall.
4 Don't try to learn anything new the night before the exam.

The Science action plan

These are the main areas that you need to cover in science. Each area is a revision unit. Use this as a route map to what you have to learn and tick your coverage as you go along. If you have only a certain amount of time before the exam, work out how quickly you need to cover the units and divide the time up. Record your progress here if you like. Then concentrate on the units you're least confident about.

You might like to start your action plan by finding out and recording:

Dates of exams

Tier (level) you're entered for Foundation / Higher Foundation (Single)

Unit	How many times revised 1	2	3	Check Up score /20	Exam Practice score	Areas in which you feel you need more practice
Biology						
1 Cells and cell activity						
2 Nutrition						
3 Respiration, breathing and gas exchange						
4 Communication and control						
5 Transport						
6 Reproduction						
7 Cell division, variation, inheritance and evolution						
8 Ecosystems						

Chemistry						
9 The structure of the atom						
10 Particles, bonding and structure						
11 Formulae, equations and calculations						
12 The periodic table						
13 The chemistry of carbon compounds						
14 Metals						
15 Rates of reaction and equilibrium						
16 Rocks of the earth and Earth cycles						
Physics						
17 Currents and circuits						
18 Charge, current and magnetism						
19 Force and pressure						
20 Force and motion						
21 Waves						
22 The Earth and beyond						
23 Energy						
24 Radioactivity						

The secrets of sucess in Science

Assuming you have planned your revision carefully, what do you have to do to succeed in the actual exams? Here are ten key points to remember:

1 It may seem obvious but make sure you put your name, centre number and candidate number clearly on the paper in the spaces provided. Very few papers go astray but mistakes do occur. Also make sure you have been given the correct paper. Every year some candidates entered for higher tier, for example, are given and complete a foundation tier paper.

2 Make sure you complete the paper. If a paper is 100 marks long and you only answer questions to score the first 80 marks you are going to greatly reduce your chances of success. Roughly, examiners expect you to spend one minute on each mark - what we call 'the mark a minute rule'. All questions are compulsory so don't spend time reading the whole paper. Start the first question. It is usually a straightforward one to help you settle down. If the question has a total of 10 marks it should take no longer than 10 minutes. If you spend longer you may be short of time later on.

3 If there is a question you are sure you can't do, leave it and move on, but write on the back page 'go back to question 4' to remind you at the end. It's easy to forget to go back, and sometimes returning to a question later helps you to do it.

4 Don't forget to answer all the questions. There are no marks deducted for wrong answers. All too often candidates either miss out a whole double page by turning over two at once or forget to turn over to the back page. Very occasionally there can be mistakes in the printing of individual papers. All the pages are numbered so check before you finish that there are no numbers missing. If there are, ask the supervisor.

5 If you are answering a biology question for example, do not be afraid to include ideas from physics and chemistry.

6 Working with equations is crucial to success at higher tier. In chemistry you should be able to write and interpret balanced equations using chemical symbols. In physics there are some key equations which you must remember and which will not be given in the paper; for example, force = mass x acceleration. Make a careful note of them as you work with this book.

7 In calculations always show your working. If you make a mistake the examiner may be able to award some of the marks available for part of the calculation being correct. If you just put down a wrong answer you have no chance of getting any marks. Always make sure your answer has the correct unit.

8 If a question is worth three marks, this should suggest to you that there are three points to be made; three marks cannot be awarded for just a single word answer. Look for three different points in your three-mark answer rather than one point expressed in three different ways. Don't worry if you can give four!

9 On all GCSE science papers 25% of the marks have to be awarded for answers requiring extended or continuous writing. This does not have to be in sentences; often a clearly drawn and labelled diagram can help your answer. When you have completed an answer requiring a couple of sentences or more, read it through slowly to yourself. Think: if you read it in a book, would it convey the information? Don't fall into the trap of thinking because you have written a lot it will impress the examiner.

10 Try to use scientific words in your answer. In some ways science is like a foreign language. It has a vocabulary which the examiner is expecting you to use. This is especially important when you are aiming for Grade B or above.

Revision Unit 1

Cells and cell activity

The Check Up

The cell

1 What is the basic unit of life? Movement, respiration, sensitivity (MRS GREN) x

2 Which life processes are missing from the following list? Movement, respiration, sensitivity, excretion ✓

Growth Nutrition Reproduction

3 Which life process releases energy from food? Nutrition x

4 Name **four** features that plant and animal cells have in common. Nucleus, cell membrane, vacuole x ½

5 Name **three** features that are peculiar to plant cells. Cell wall, chloroplasts ½

6 What name is given to a collection of cells of the same type? Tissue ✓

7 Which of the following is an organ? Liver ✓

Neurone Liver Gut

8 Name **two** human organ systems. Reproductive and digestive x

9 What is meant by the term partially permeable? A partially permeable cell lets some substances through. ✓

10 Name a partially permeable cytoplasmic membrane. Stem x

11 In **one** word, how would you describe the way particles move in liquids and gases? Diffusion x

12 By which process does oxygen leave the lung air space to enter the blood? Absorption x

13 Diffusion is described as a passive process. What does this mean? It is constant x

14 Cell A contains a higher concentration of an ion than an adjacent cell, cell B. In which direction will net movement of the ion take place by diffusion? Upwards x

15 What must separate two solutions for osmosis to take place? Active transport x

16 What determines the direction of net movement of water osmotically?

What type of cell the cell is x

17 Water leaves the soil and enters the cellulose wall of a root hair cell. From there it passes into the cytoplasm of the cell.

a Which process is involved in the movement into the wall? Diffusion ✓

b Which process is responsible for the movement of water into the cytoplasm? Active transport x

18 Under what circumstances does osmotic equilibrium occur with respect to two adjacent cells?

x

19 When is active transport necessary for the movement of particles?

x

20 What is the link between respiration and active transport?

x

Mark yourself *(see answers on page 106)*

- More than 12? Do the exam practice – or go on to another unit.
- Less than 12? Do the crash course on the next page.

6/20

THE CRASH COURSE

Life processes

Plants and animals have **seven** life processes in common:

Movement, **R**espiration, **S**ensitivity, **G**rowth, **R**eproduction, **E**xcretion and **N**utrition.

To help you remember:
MRS GREN

Cells

Plant and animal cells have many features in common, but also have several important differences.

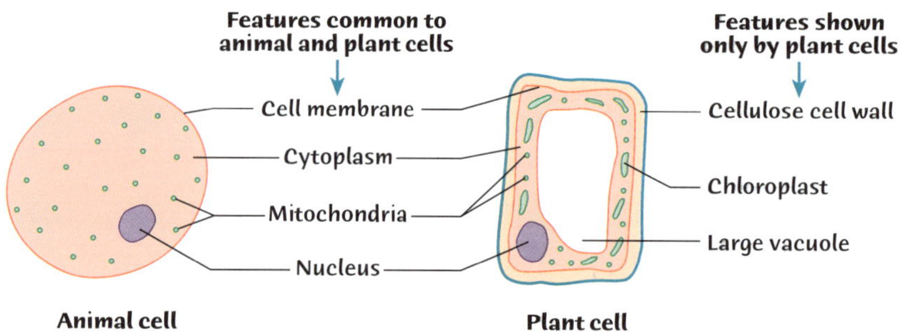

Tissues, organs and organ systems

Many-celled organisms show a variety of types of **cells** each **adapted** to carry out a particular **function**.

A group of cells of the same type working together to carry out a particular function is known as a **tissue**.

A group of tissues working together forms an **organ**.

Groups of organs form **organ systems**.

An **organ system** shows **adaptations** that enable it to play a part in a **particular life process**.

Level	Examples
Cells	Sperm, neurone, stomatal guard cell, palisade mesophyll cell
Tissues	Muscle, blood, phloem, xylem
Organs	Heart, liver, leaf, stamen
Organ systems	Alimentary canal, cardiovascular, root, shoot

THE CRASH COURSE

Cell membranes

A cytoplasmic membrane is found at the surface of all living cells.

This membrane is **partially permeable**.

Small molecules and ions may pass through partially permeable membranes but larger molecules do so only slowly or not at all.

Diffusion

Diffusion is one result of the **random motion** that particles show.

Where there is a difference in concentration, more particles leave the area of higher concentration than enter it in any fixed period of time.

The **net movement** of particles is **down** the **concentration gradient**, **from** the region of **higher** concentration **to** that of **lower** concentration.

At **equilibrium**, the two concentrations are the **same** and the number of particles being exchanged between the two regions in any fixed period of time is the same.

Diffusion is a **passive** process. This means it is a process that does not require an energy supply.

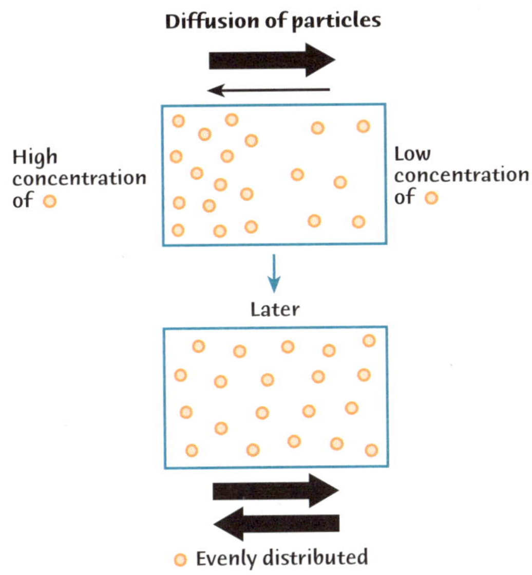

Osmosis

Partially permeable membranes in living cells allow a special form of diffusion to take place. It is known as **osmosis**.

In living cells, osmosis is concerned with the **diffusion of water molecules**.

Water molecules diffuse from a region of **higher water** concentration, **to** one of **lower water** concentration through a partially permeable membrane.

Remember that water diffuses in **both** directions across a cell membrane. The **net result** depends on the steepness and direction of the water diffusion gradient.

At **equilibrium**, the two water concentrations are the same and the number of water molecules being exchanged through the membrane in any fixed period of time is the same.

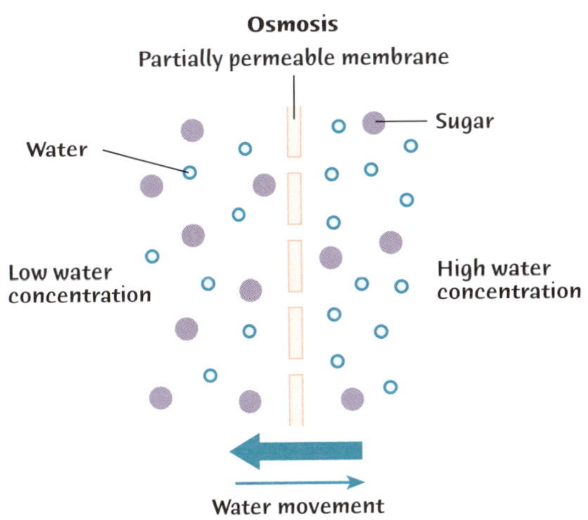

Active transport

There are situations in living systems where molecules and ions enter or leave cells **against** a **concentration gradient** by **active transport**.

Active transport is an **energy requiring** process.

Energy is provided by **respiration**.

Exam Practice

1

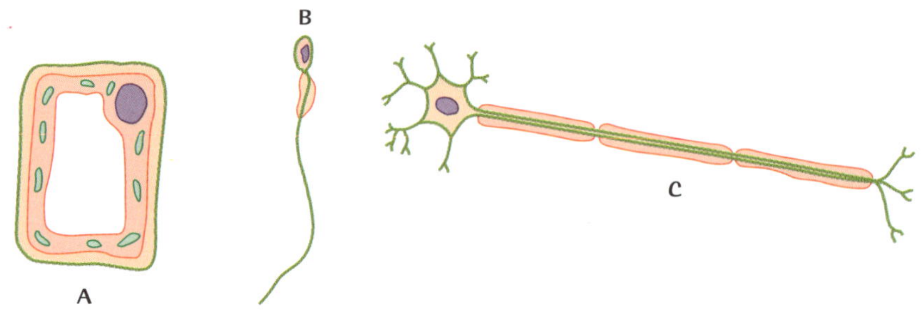

a List **three** structural features shown by cell **A** that identify it as a plant cell. 3 marks

b Cells **B** and **C** show differences in structure.

How are the cells adapted to their particular function? 2 marks

2 a Uncooked potato chips are sometimes placed in a bowl of cold tap water to keep them fresh until they are to be cooked.

Uncooked chips prepared in this way are much harder and stiffer than raw chips not placed in water before they are used.

Give an explanation for this difference. 8 marks

b Cooked potatoes, cooled in tap water, remain relatively soft and flexible.

Explain why cooked and raw potatoes behave differently with respect to water. 2 marks

3 a In which direction does diffusion naturally occur? 1 mark

The table shows the results of an investigation into the absorption of mineral nutrients from the soil by the roots of a plant.

Mineral nutrient	External concentration (mM)	Internal concentration (mM)	Percentage increase (%)
Calcium ion	0.2	5.0	2500
Chloride ion	1.2	27.0	2250
Potassium ion	1.0	22.0	2200

b Which of the three ions recorded in the table shows the steepest concentration gradient? 1 mark

c Explain the results for the absorption of potassium ions by the plant involved. 4 marks

d i) Which ion is absorbed the most effectively? 1 mark

ii) What does this suggest about this plant's ability to absorb these three ions from the soil? 3 marks

Revision Unit 2

Nutrition

The Check Up

1 What is the source of energy found in all plant and animal food? ______

2 Write down an equation for photosynthesis using words and symbols.

______

3 Name the pigment essential for photosynthesis. ______

4 List **three** factors that would limit the rate of photosynthesis of a given surface area of a green leaf.

______

5 Which colour or colours of the spectrum for white light are most effective in photosynthesis? ______

6 Which colour of light is least effective in photosynthesis? ______

7 Name **one** element that plants have to absorb as a mineral ion from the soil or water around them in order to make proteins. ______

8 The human diet includes carbohydrates, proteins, dietary fibre and water. Name **three** other essential dietary components. ______

9 What is meant by the term 'balanced diet'? ______

______

10 The following processes are associated with the treatment of food by the human gut but they are not in the correct sequence. Write down the letters **A–E** in the correct order.

A absorption **B** assimilation **C** digestion **D** egestion **E** ingestion ______

11 What is meant by the term ingestion? ______

12 Complete the following word equation by naming the enzyme and the product:

starch —(*enzyme*)→ *product*

13 Where is hydrochloric acid secreted into the gut? ______

14 Give **two** functions for the hydrochloric acid secreted into the gut. ______

15 What is the function of bile? ______

16 In which part of the gut are polypeptides converted into amino acids? ______

17 Name the end products of fat digestion. ______

18 Give **three** features of the small intestine that create a very large surface area for absorption.

______

19 How are simple sugars and amino acids taken away from the small intestine for use elsewhere? ______

20 What is a lacteal? ______

Mark yourself *(see answers on page 106)*

- More than 12? Do the exam practice – or go on to another unit.
- Less than 12? Do the crash course on the next page.

/20

THE CRASH COURSE

Plant nutrition – photosynthesis

Plants produce sugar by **photosynthesis**. This provides **energy** for the plants and for animals that feed on them.

The equation for photosynthesis is:

$$\underset{\text{carbon dioxide}}{6CO_2} + \underset{\text{water}}{6H_2O} \longrightarrow \underset{\text{glucose}}{C_6H_{12}O_6} + \underset{\text{oxygen}}{6O_2}$$

The energy required for photosynthesis is provided by **sunlight**. A green pigment, **chlorophyll**, absorbs sunlight. Only plants with this pigment can photosynthesise.

Rate of photosynthesis

Photosynthesis in a plant is affected by the:

- amount of light available
- concentration of carbon dioxide
- temperature.

If the amount of light is low, but the concentration of carbon dioxide and the temperature are suitable, photosynthesis is slowed down. Light is described as a **limiting factor**.

The rate of photosynthesis is affected by light in two ways. The rate is affected by light intensity (quantity) and wavelength (colour). **Blue and red light** are absorbed and used in photosynthesis; **green** light is reflected.

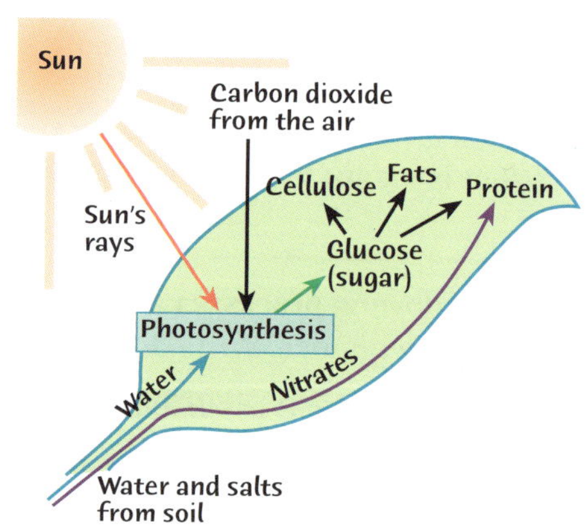

Products of photosynthesis

Plants use the sugar made by photosynthesis to make other substances for their and dependent animal use.

Carbon dioxide and water provide the elements carbon, hydrogen and oxygen. Nitrogen is needed to make amino acids and proteins. This and other elements required by plants are absorbed as **mineral ions** from the water or soil around the plants.

Human nutrition

The human **diet** contains:

- carbohydrates
- fats
- proteins
- vitamins
- mineral salts
- dietary fibre
- water.

A **balanced diet** must include all the foods listed above for growth and repair, enough energy and essential health factors to meet the needs of the **individual** concerned.

The organ system involved in the treatment of food is the **alimentary canal** (gut).

The alimentary canal is a continuous tube, **modified** along its length, to carry out specific functions.

Functions of the alimentary canal:

- Ingestion (capture)
- Digestion
- Absorption
- Assimilation
- Egestion

THE CRASH COURSE

Digestion and absorption

Food molecules in the alimentary canal must be **absorbed** before they can be of use to the cells.

Food must be **digested** before it can be absorbed.

Digestion	Agent	Activity
Mechanical	Teeth	Chewing
Chemical	Enzymes	Hydrolysis

An **enzyme** works best at a particular pH. Different parts of the gut have different pHs. For example, the stomach contains **hydrochloric acid** that not only provides the **optimum** (best) pH for the enzymes working there but also sterilises material that enters the stomach.

Bile salts added to the contents of the duodenum emulsify the fats present.

Food at start	After digestion
Carbohydrates	Simple sugars
Fats	Fatty acids and glycerol
Proteins	Amino acids

The **small intestine** is **adapted** for **absorption**.

Features of the small intestine that make it good at absorbing food and distributing it after digestion	
Considerable length (about 6 metres) Folding of inner surface Villi and microvilli	Very large surface area for the absorption of digested food
Good supply of blood and lymph	Rapid removal of absorbed food to other parts of the body

Continued ▶

THE CRASH COURSE

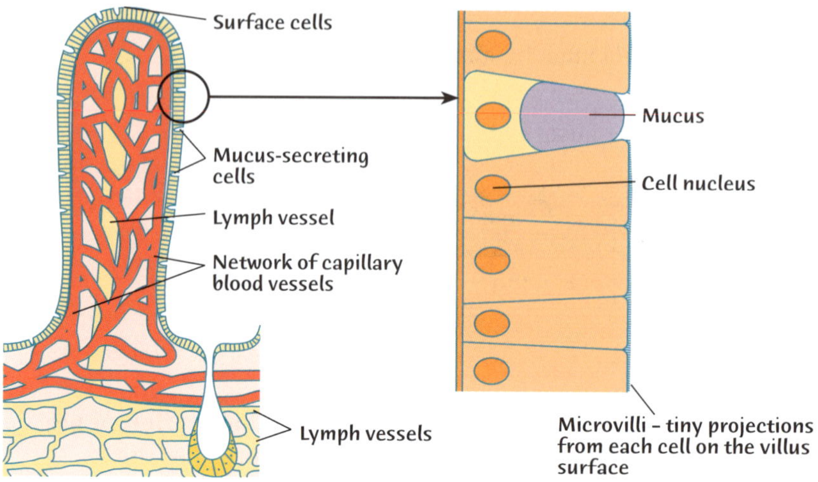

Inside a villus and part of its surface

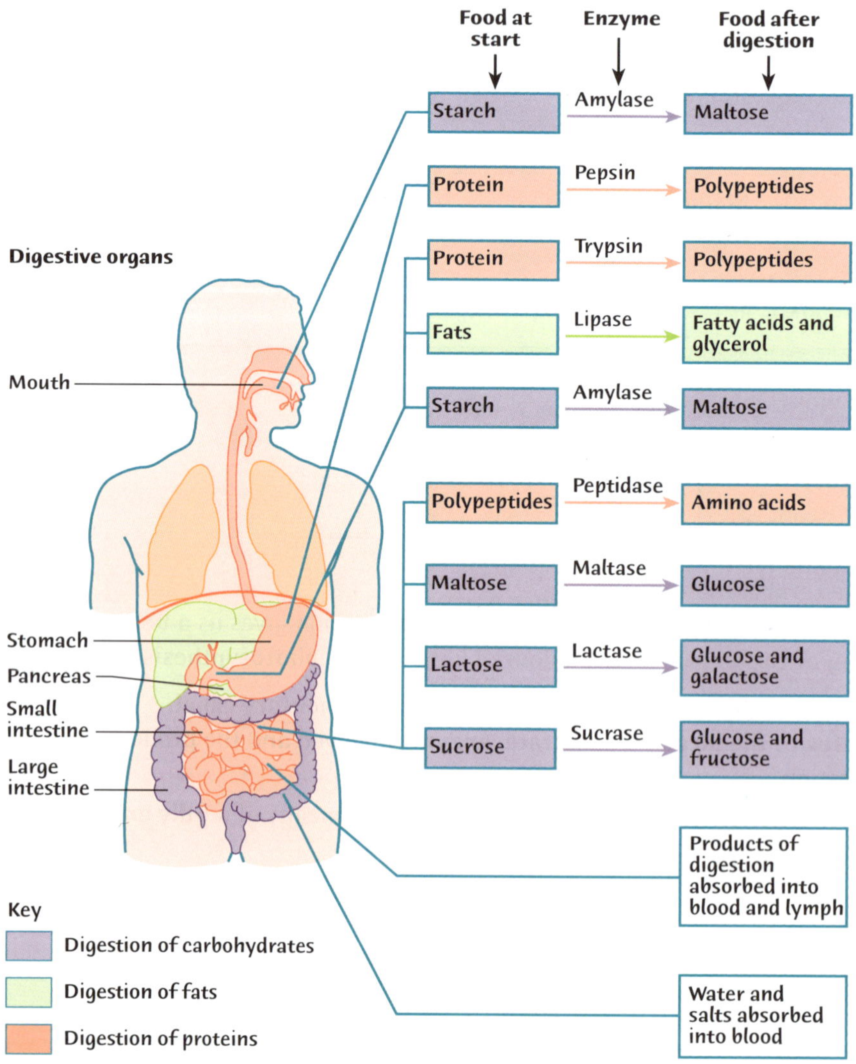

Digestion and absorption in the human gut

N.B. The names of most enzymes end in **-ase**.

EXAM PRACTICE

1 a i) Add symbols for the reactant and product to complete a balanced equation summarising photosynthesis. **2 marks**

[ ] + $6H_2O$ $\longrightarrow$ [ ] + $6O_2$

ii) **Two** important features of photosynthesis are missing from the summary. What are they? **2 marks**

b An experiment to investigate the effectiveness of different wavelengths of light for photosynthesis was carried out in 1883 by a German botanist called Engelmann. He used a filamentous green alga, aerobic bacteria and light that had been passed through a prism.

Wavelength of light (nm)	Colour of light
450	Blue
550	Green
580	Yellow
675	Red

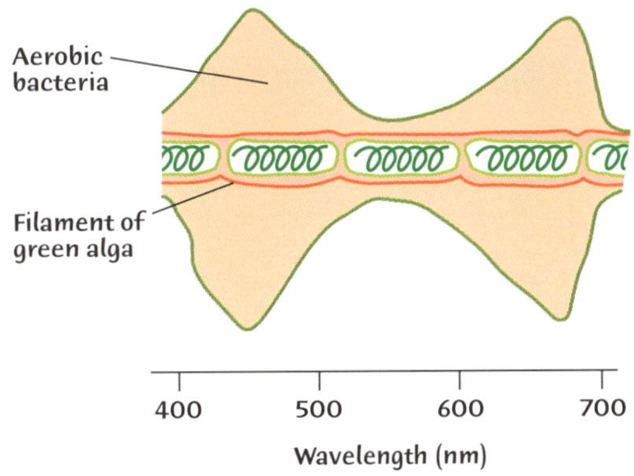

i) The aerobic bacteria appear to congregate in two places along the filament. At which wavelengths of light did Engelmann observe the highest numbers of bacteria in each of these areas?

What was the colour of the light at each of these peaks? **4 marks**

Wavelength (nm)	Colour of light

ii) What does the term aerobic mean? **1 mark**

iii) Explain how the distribution of bacteria in this investigation gives us a better understanding of the way different coloured light affects photosynthesis. **5 marks**

2 a Describe the complete digestion of starch in the human alimentary canal. At each stage refer to the location, substrate, enzyme involved and the product or products of digestion. **6 marks**

b Describe in detail the structure and function of a villus by means of a fully annotated diagram. **5 marks**

The Check Up

1 What are the usual reactants for aerobic respiration?

2 Name the waste product of anaerobic respiration in muscle cells.

3 Write the word equation for anaerobic respiration in yeast.

4 Name **two** ways in which people use anaerobic respiration carried out by yeast.

5 What effect does lactic acid have on muscle function?

6 What is meant by the term 'oxygen debt'?

7 List the following food chemicals in order of decreasing energy content per gram:

carbohydrate fat protein

8 What is ATP and what is it used for?

9 Name the parts **A–E** on the diagram. **A**

B

C

D

E

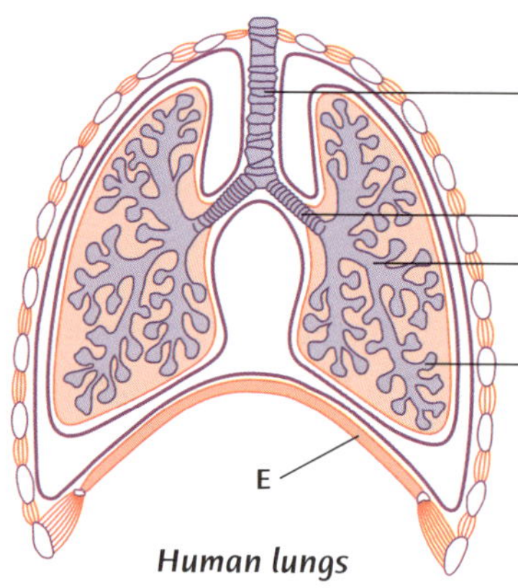

Human lungs

10 List **five** features of an efficient gas exchange surface.

11 Where does the exchange of gases occur in the human lung?

12 Name the blood vessel that carries blood to the lungs from the heart.

13 How does oxygen get from the lung air space to the blood at the gas exchange surface?

14 Describe the concentration gradient for carbon dioxide at the gas exchange surface of the lung.

15 How are the concentration gradients for carbon dioxide and oxygen maintained at the gas exchange surface of the lung?

16 What will happen to the rate of respiration when someone exercises?

17 Why do athletes show raised ventilation rates long after their exercise has finished?

18 Where are the centres that automatically control the breathing rate?

19 What are respiratory centres sensitive to?

20 How does information from the respiratory centres reach the structures involved in breathing?

Mark yourself *(see answers on page 107)*

- More than 12? Do the exam practice – or go on to another unit.
- Less than 12? Do the crash course on the next page.

/20

The Crash Course

Respiration

Respiration releases energy from carbohydrates, fats and proteins. **Glucose** is the most commonly respired compound.

Aerobic respiration:

Glucose + Oxygen → Carbon dioxide + Water + Energy

Anaerobic respiration in **plants**:

Glucose → Carbon dioxide + Ethanol + Energy

Anaerobic respiration in yeast is known as **fermentation** and is employed in bread-making and the manufacture of alcoholic drinks such as wine and beer.

Anaerobic respiration in **animals** and some bacteria:

Glucose → Lactic acid + Energy

Lactic acid causes **muscle fatigue**.

Sustained anaerobic respiration in humans leads to an accumulation of lactic acid. This creates an **oxygen debt** that has to be 'repaid' once aerobic conditions have been restored.

NB raised ventilation rates are present in athletes long after their exercise has finished.

Aerobic respiration releases much **more energy** than anaerobic respiration from the same amount of glucose. Ethanol (waste product of anaerobic respiration) still releases energy when it burns.

Different food chemicals release different quantities of energy when they are respired.

Food	Energy per gram (kJ)
Carbohydrate	17.2
Fat	38.5
Protein	22.2

The energy released during respiration is used to produce **adenosine triphosphate** (ATP). **ATP** is used to transfer the energy necessary for chemical changes to take place in a living cell.

Breathing and gas exchange

Breathing

Inhaled **air** contains a **mixture of gases** including oxygen, carbon dioxide, nitrogen and water vapour.

	Approximate composition as a percentage of volume	
Gas	Inhaled air	Exhaled air
oxygen	21	14
carbon dioxide	0.04	3.8
water vapour	1.2	6.2
nitrogen	78	76

Pathway for respiratory gases

Air
Nose and mouth
Trachea
Bronchi
Bronchioles
Alveoli
Blood

Continued ▶

The Crash Course

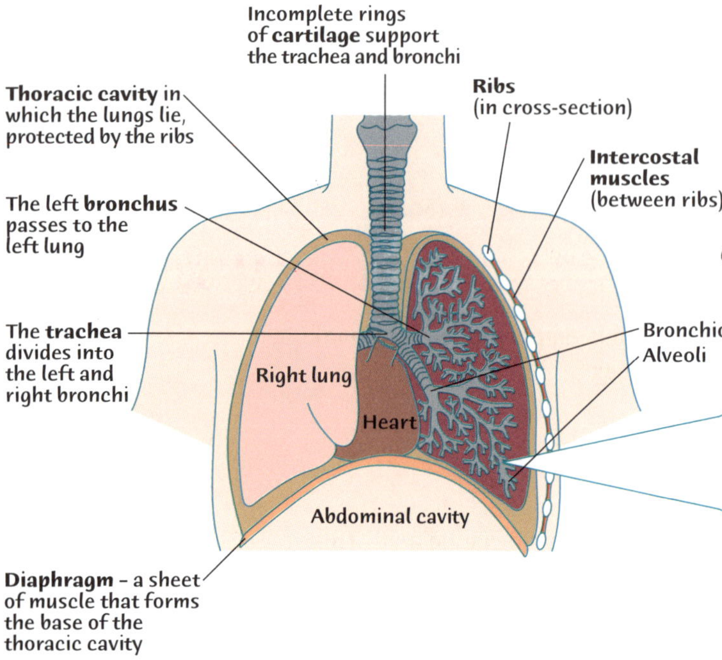

The lungs in the human body

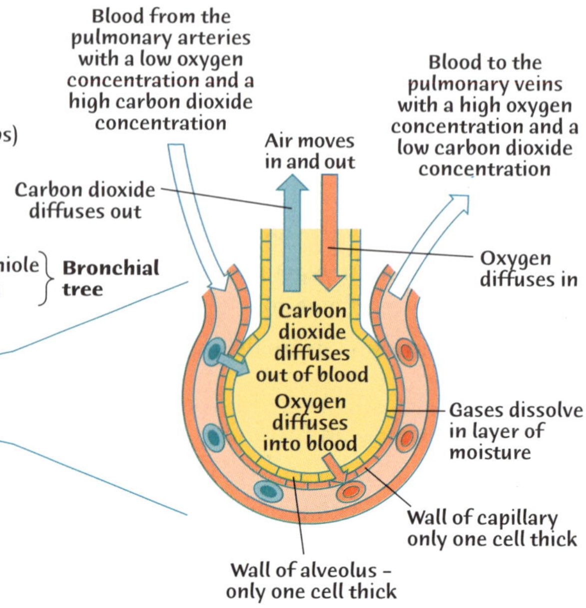

Section through an alveolus showing gas exchange

Gas exchange

The alveoli (air sacs) form an efficient **gas exchange surface** because they:

- are moist;
- have very thin walls;
- are permeable to gases in solution;
- together offer a very large surface area (approximately 90 m^2);
- are close to an efficient blood supply.

Continuous ventilation of the lungs (breathing) and blood circulation maintain the concentration gradients for the exchange of carbon dioxide and oxygen at the gas exchange surface.

Rate of respiration **varies** according to the energy demands of the organism. Blood oxygen and carbon dioxide concentrations will therefore vary. **Homeostatic control** centres in the brain, which are sensitive to blood concentrations of carbon dioxide and lactic acid, monitor their concentrations.

Control of breathing rate

Increased rate of respiration

↓

Increased blood carbon dioxide concentration

↓

Respiratory centres (RCs) in the brain register the increase

↓

Nerve impulses sent from RCs to diaphragm and intercostal muscles

↓

Breathing rate raised

↓

Blood carbon dioxide concentration returns to normal

The Crash Course

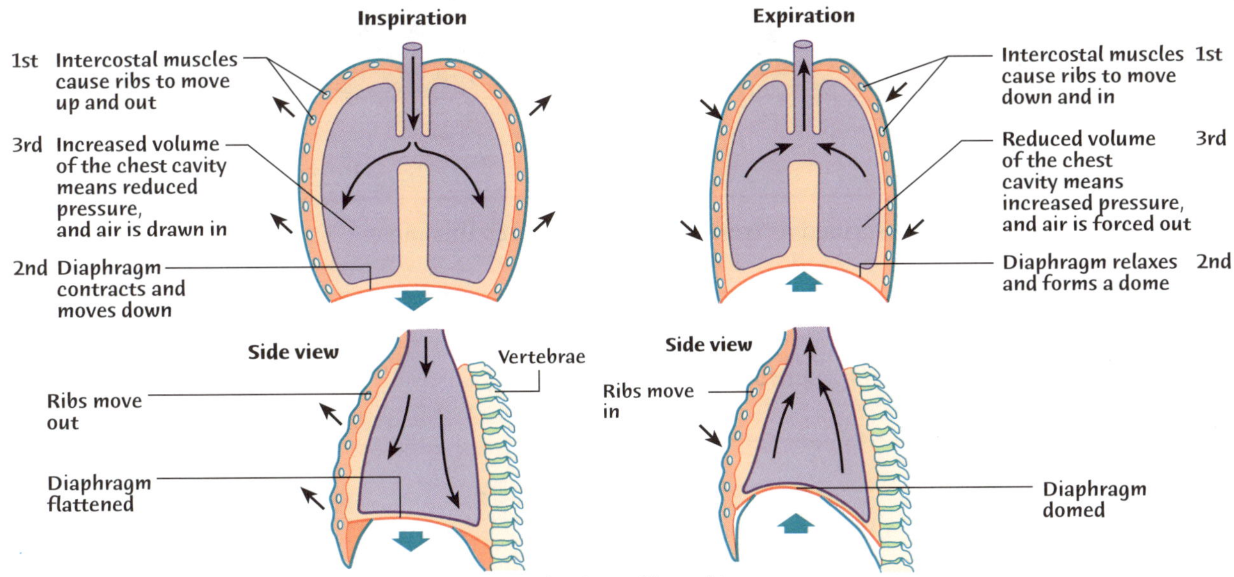

Mechanism of breathing

Exam Practice

1 a The following word equation for aerobic respiration of glucose is incomplete.

Glucose + A ⟶ B + water + energy

i) Complete the word equation for the aerobic respiration of 1 mol of glucose. **2 marks**

ii) Some of the energy released during aerobic respiration is released as heat.
A cell cannot use heat to power its life processes.
In what form is 'usable energy' made available to the cell? **1 mark**

iii) Give **one** way in which the overall change would have differed if 1 mol of fat had been respired instead of glucose. **1 mark**

b How is anaerobic respiration in yeast involved in the manufacture of bread? **4 marks**

c i) How will the respiration taking place in an athlete's muscles at the end of a 100 m sprint be different from what was going on at the start? **1 mark**

ii) Explain why the change referred to in i) takes place and the consequences of the change. **6 marks**

2 a Air passes through the following structures on its way from the atmosphere **into** the lungs. They are not in the correct order.

A alveoli **B** bronchi **C** bronchioles **D** nose **E** trachea

List the letters **A–E** in the correct order. **4 marks**

b Explain how the mechanical process of breathing causes air to **enter** the lungs. **5 marks**

c Respiration causes the concentration of gases in solution in the blood to change. Respiratory centres in the brain monitor changes in the blood's composition. Which gas in particular do they monitor? **1 mark**

Revision Unit 4

Communication and control

The Check Up

1 Name six senses. ____________________

2 Sense organs are sometimes described as transducers. What does this mean?

____

3 What is an effector? ____________________

4 Label **A**, **B** and **C** on the diagram of a sensory neurone.

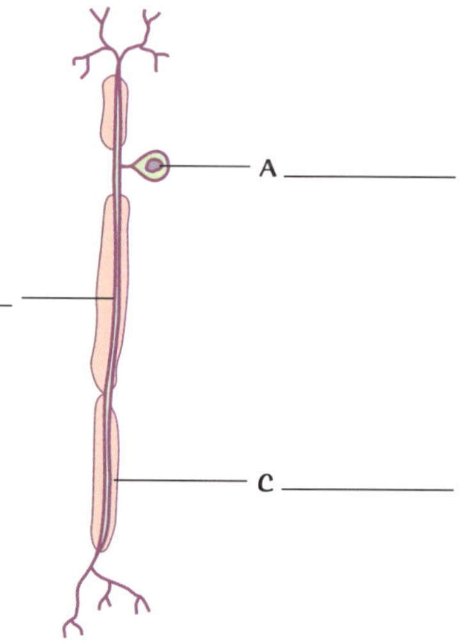

Sensory neurone

5 What is a synapse? ____________________

____

6 What term is used to describe sneezing, blinking or knee jerk?

____

7 How do hormonal glands differ from glands such as the tear gland?

____

8 Which gland produces insulin? ____________________

9 What is the function of insulin? ____________________

10 Name a male sex hormone. ____________________

11 Where is oestrogen produced? ____________________

12 Name **two** hormones involved in the human menstrual cycle.

____________ and ____________

13 What does the term 'homeostasis' mean? ____________________

____

14 Name **two** organs involved in the control of blood glucose concentration.

____________ and ____________

15 Which part of the human kidney carries out selective reabsorption of water?

____

16 Which hormone plays a part in controlling the reabsorption of water in the kidney? ____________

17 How does the raising and lowering of body hair affect the amount of heat lost from the body surface?

____

18 What does the term 'vasodilation' mean? ____________________

19 Name a plant hormone. ____________________

20 Gardeners may use plant hormones artificially. Name one gardening product that contains plant hormones.

____

Mark yourself *(see answers on page 108)*

- More than 12? Do the exam practice – or go on to another unit.
- Less than 12? Do the crash course on the next page.

/20

The Crash Course

Nervous system

The human body possesses a number of receptors, **sensors**, that enable it to detect change in factors, **stimuli**, in the environment, e.g. light and sound.

Stimulus	Sensor	Sense
Light	Eye	Sight
Sound	Ear	Hearing
Gravity/movement	Ear	Balance
Chemical	Nose/tongue	Smell/taste
Pressure/pain	Skin	Touch

Sensors, e.g. eye and ear, are **transducers** that transform the energy of a stimulus into nerve impulses.

Nerve impulses initiated by sense organs bring about change in **effectors**, i.e. a tissue, an organ or a gland.

Three types of nerve cell (neurone) are involved in the transmission of impulses:
- sensory,
- relay (intermediate) and
- motor.

Remember:
- Nerve cells are not connected directly to one another.
- Enzymes control the production or removal of transmitter substances in gaps called synapses.
- The sequence in nervous transmission is:
  Stimulus
  Sensor
  Nerves – sensory
  relay
  motor
  Effectors
  Response

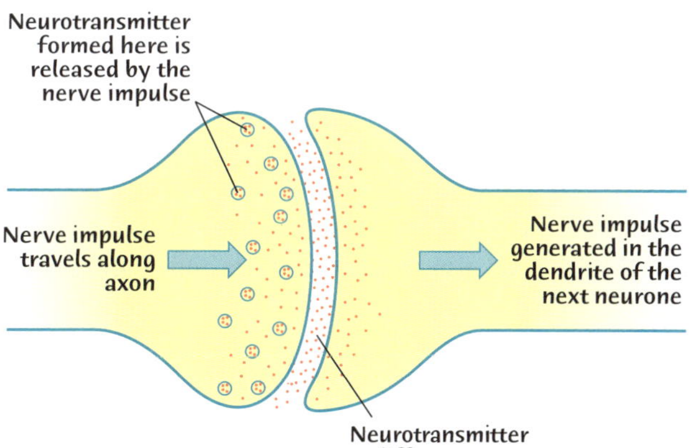

A synapse

Reflexes enable rapid response to stimuli without the brain being involved in a conscious way.

Examples of cranial reflex (relay neurone in the brain)	Examples of spinal reflex (relay neurone in the spinal cord)
Blinking	Knee-jerk
Constriction of the iris	Withdrawal of limb

THE CRASH COURSE

Human hormonal system

Hormonal glands have no ducts. They release chemical messengers called **hormones** into the blood stream.

Communication	
Hormonal	Nervous
Chemical	Electrical
Slow	Very fast
Long lasting	Brief
Causes a more general effect	Has a very specific effect

Hormonal gland	Hormone	Function
Pancreas	Insulin	Involved in the feedback mechanism that controls the concentration of blood glucose. Promotes the conversion of glucose to glycogen in the liver
Testis	Testosterone	Controls the development of the male sex organs and, at puberty, the male secondary sexual characteristics
Ovary	Oestrogen Progesterone	Control the development of the female sex organs and, at puberty, the female secondary sexual characteristics including the menstrual cycle

Remember:

- **Diabetes** occurs when the pancreas is not producing enough insulin. It can be remedied by injection of insulin.
- Medically, female sex hormones can be used, in a controlled manner, either as a contraceptive method to **control fertility** or conversely to **enhance it**.

THE CRASH COURSE

Plant hormones

Plants produce hormones that help to control their growth and development. **Auxins** influence the patterns of growth seen in **phototropism** (response to light) and **geotropism** (response to gravity).

Examples of the artificial application of plant hormones include their use in '**rooting powders**', some **selective weedkillers** and in the production of **seedless fruit**.

Homeostasis

Homeostasis is the maintenance of a stable environment.
Systems exist in the human body to enable this to occur allowing cells to operate in **optimal** (best) **conditions**.

Examples include the maintenance of: blood glucose concentration
body water content
body temperature.

Insulin promotes the removal of **glucose** from the blood and its conversion, by the **liver**, to glycogen.

Feedback mechanism to control the secretion of insulin:

1. High blood glucose concentration
2. promotes the release of more insulin by the **pancreas**.
3. More blood glucose is converted to glycogen by liver cells.
4. This lowers the blood glucose concentration.
5. Therefore the pancreas releases less insulin.
6. Therefore less glucose is converted to glycogen by liver cells.

NB Glucagon, another hormone released by the pancreas, promotes the conversion of glycogen to glucose.

Selective reabsorption of **water** in the **kidney tubules** helps to maintain water balance.

1. When blood water concentration falls the pituitary gland (in the brain) releases anti-diuretic hormone (ADH).
2. ADH affects the permeability of the kidney tubules. Release of ADH into the blood stream leads to the reabsorption of more water. Less is lost in urine.
3. Blood water concentration rises so less ADH is released and more water is lost in urine.

The **skin** functions as a homeostatic organ to control **body temperature** in three ways.

1. The hairs can be raised or lowered increasing or decreasing **insulation**.
2. **Evaporation of sweat** produced in glands in the skin leads to loss of heat from underlying tissue.
3. **Changes in the flow** of blood through skin capillaries affect the volume of blood cooled at the surface. **Vasodilation** (expansion of blood vessels) leads to increased blood flow and heat loss. **Vasoconstriction** (contraction of blood vessels) leads to the converse.

Exam Practice

1

Sense	Stimulus	Sense organ
Hearing	**A**	Ear
Smell	**B**	Nose
Balance	**C**	**D**

a Name stimuli **A**, **B** and **C**. 3 marks

b Name sense organ **D**. 1 mark

c The human retina contains **two** different types of light sensitive cells.
Describe how these cells are distributed in the retina and their role in human vision. 6 marks

2 Describe how one nerve cell communicates with the next at a synapse. 5 marks

3 Structures **A–E** are involved in a reflex arc.

A Effector
B Motor neurone
C Relay neurone
D Sensor
E Sensory neurone

a List the letters **A–E** in the correct sequence for a reflex arc. 4 marks

b Blinking and the knee jerk response are two examples of reflex action in humans.
Where will the relay neurones be for the two reflex arcs?
i) Blinking 1 mark
ii) Knee jerk 1 mark

4 Osmoreceptors in the brain monitor the water content of the blood plasma. If the concentration of water falls below normal, anti-diuretic hormone (ADH) is secreted.

a Where precisely are the target cells for ADH? 1 mark

b i) What effect does ADH have on its target cells? 1 mark
ii) What effect does this have on the composition of the blood plasma? 1 mark
iii) What effect does this have on the secretion of ADH? 1 mark

Revision Unit 5

Transport

The Check Up

1 What is the function of the pulmonary system? ______

2 Which blood vessel empties into the right atrium? ______

3 What causes the tricuspid valve to open? ______

4 How do the walls of the left ventricle differ from those of the right ventricle? ______

5 Which blood vessel carries blood away from the left ventricle? ______

6 The diagram shows a cross-section through a blood vessel.

Name the type of vessel and give **two** reasons for your answer. ______

______

______

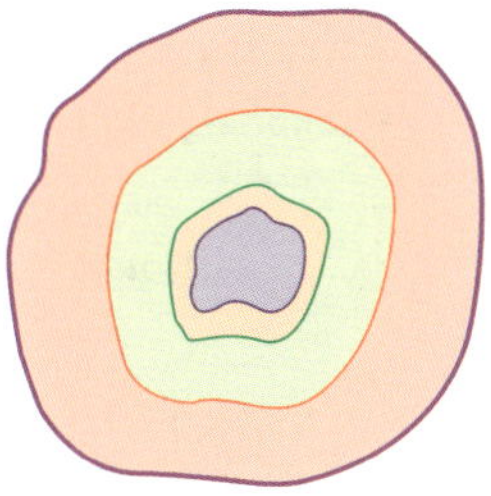

Cross-section through a blood vessel

7 What makes a blood capillary an efficient site for exchange of substances?

______

______

8 Name **two** solutes transported in the blood plasma. ______ and ______

9 Give **two** functions of white blood cells. ______ and ______

10 Which type of blood cell carries oxygen? ______

11 What is the origin of blood platelets? ______

12 Red blood cells have two concave surfaces. What significance does this have for the efficiency of the cell?

______

13 Where, in general, in the human body would you expect oxyhaemoglobin to release its oxygen?

______

14 Label **A** and **B** on the diagram of a vascular bundle.

15 Name the substance in the walls of xylem cells that makes them waterproof.

______

16 What name is given to the process of water and mineral salt transport in plants?

______

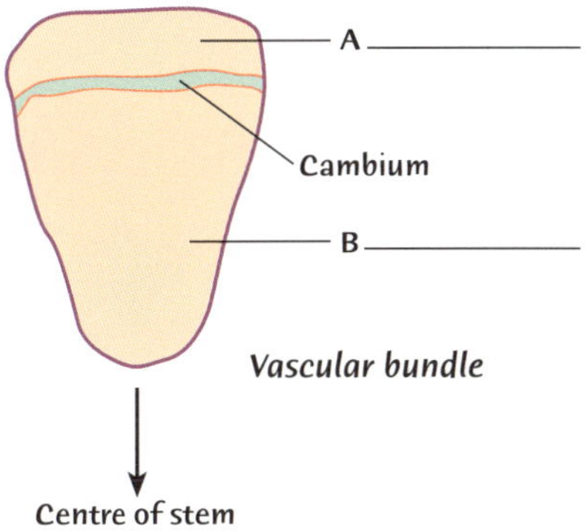

Vascular bundle

17 What is photosynthetic glucose converted to before being transported in the phloem? ______

18 How does water get into root hair cells? ______

19 Name the pores through which water is lost from the surface of leaves. ______

20 What effect would an increase in atmospheric relative humidity have on the rate of transpiration?

______

Mark yourself *(see answers on page 108)*

- More than 12? Do the exam practice – or go on to another unit.
- Less than 12? Do the crash course on the next page.

/20

THE CRASH COURSE

Transport in humans

Humans have a **double circulatory system**.

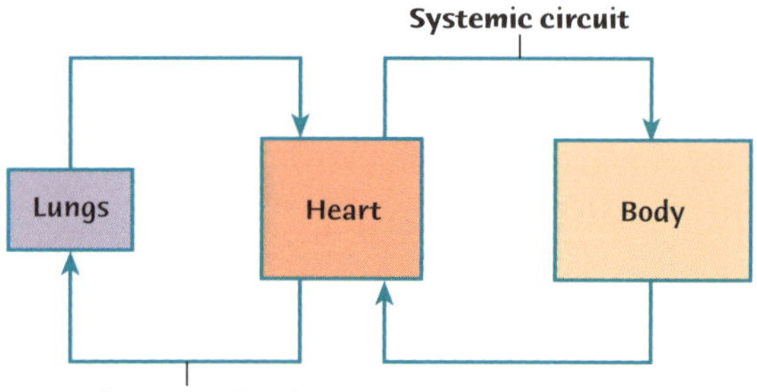

Double circulatory system

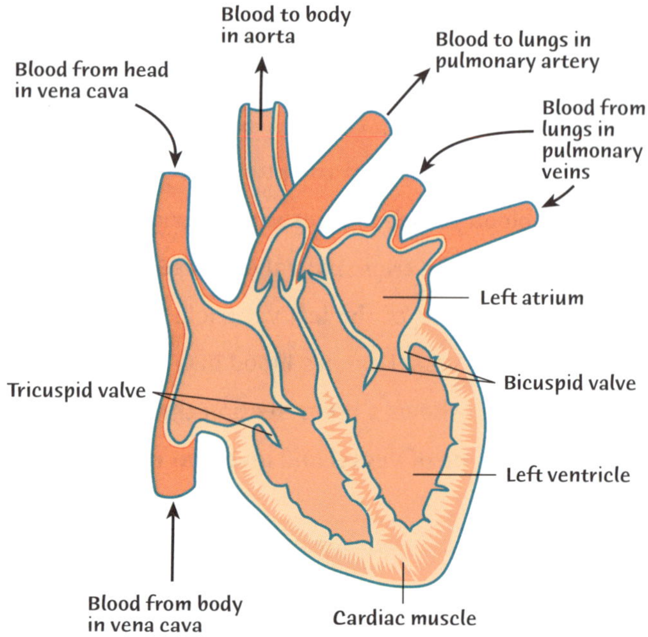

Structure of the human heart

Blood vessel	Structure	Function
Arteries	Thick wall with a lot of elastic tissue	Carry blood under pressure away from the heart
Veins	Thin wall with little elastic tissue	Carry blood back to the heart from the organs of the body at a lower pressure
Capillaries	Wall one cell thick	Link the arteries to the veins and enable the exchange of materials between the blood and the cells to take place

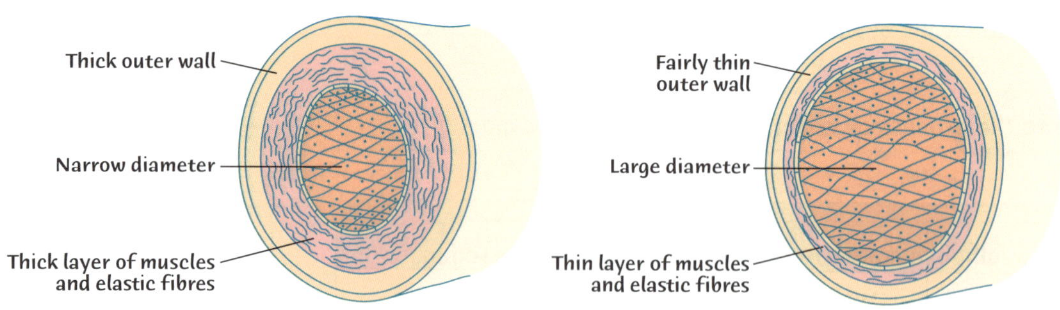

Arteries and veins compared. The smooth lining to the vessels helps blood flow and prevents clots from forming.

Remember:
- Arteries do not have valves whereas veins have pocket valves to prevent the backflow of blood likely to occur with blood at a lower pressure.
- Gaps occur between some cells in the wall of a capillary. These allow tissue fluid to escape and re-enter the capillary. This makes exchange, between the blood and cells of tissues nearby, more easy.

The Crash Course

Blood structure and function

Blood component	Function
Plasma	Solvent for materials to be transported and transport medium for larger insoluble components such as cells
Red blood cell	Contains haemoglobin. Transports oxygen
White blood cells	Different types have different functions. Some ingest bacteria and other cell debris. Others produce specific antibodies
Blood **platelets**	These are broken down red blood cells involved in the formation of clots

1 Mature red blood cells have no nucleus.
2 They have a cell membrane that is very thin and is permeable to oxygen that diffuses easily through it.
3 Red cells are biconcave, thus offering an enlarged surface area for oxygen exchange.
4 They are small and flexible, which means that they can pass through very narrow capillaries.

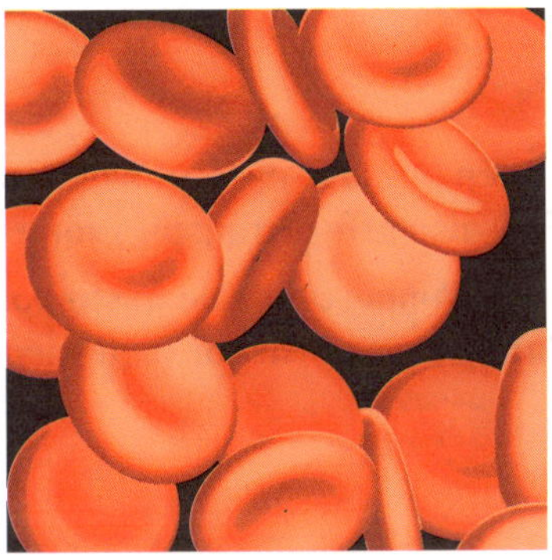

Red blood cells

Haemoglobin will react with oxygen to form **oxyhaemoglobin**. The reaction is reversible.

Oxygen + Haemoglobin ⇌ Oxyhaemoglobin

(forward: Area of oxygen supply, e.g. lungs; reverse: Area of oxygen demand, e.g. active muscle)

Transport in plants

Tissue	Mature cells	Function
Xylem	Dead	• Walls contain lignin – makes them waterproof and stronger. • Conduction – transport of water and mineral salts **up** the plant. • Support
Phloem	Alive	Translocation – movement of sucrose and other organic compounds **up and down** the plant

Continued ▶

THE CRASH COURSE

Transpiration

Water enters the roots of plants, by osmosis, from the dilute solution present in the soil.

Water moves into the root generating an upward pressure.

This, **root pressure**, pushes water and dissolved mineral nutrients, from the root xylem up into the xylem of the stem.

Water evaporates from leaf air spaces into the atmosphere through the **stomata** (pores in the leaf). This causes water to be dragged from the leaf xylem and in turn from the stem xylem.

This process is known as **transpiration**.

Factors that affect evaporation also affect the rate of transpiration, e.g.

- temperature
- relative humidity
- air movement.

Remember

- **Stomata** can open or close in response to changes in environmental conditions. They also affect transpiration rate.
- Water plays a very important role in support, particularly for herbaceous, non-woody plants. Loss of **turgor** (cell vacuole water pressure) leads to wilting.

EXAM PRACTICE

Double circulation in a mammal

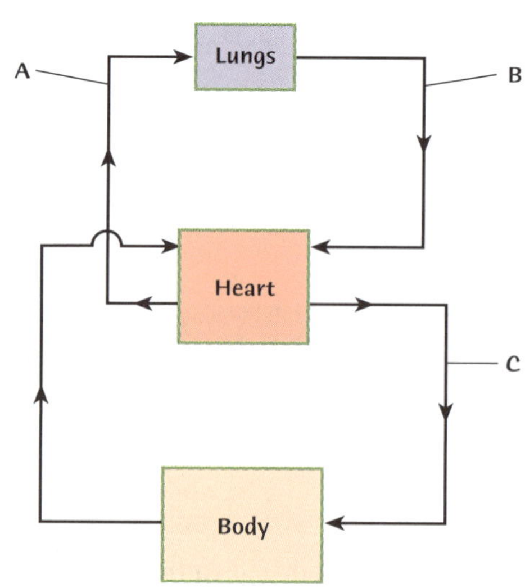

1 a i) Name blood vessels **A** and **B**. (2 marks)
ii) How will the composition of blood in blood vessel **B** differ from that in **A**? (2 marks)
iii) Explain your answer to ii). (2 marks)

b What name is given to the circuit that includes the heart and the body? (1 mark)

c i) How will blood pressure in vessel **C** differ from that in **A**? (1 mark)
ii) Explain your answer to i). (2 marks)

2 Describe the pathway of blood from the point where it enters the **left-hand** side of the heart, to the point where it leaves, in the aorta.
Outline the function of each of the structures that you mention. (8 marks)

3 Movement of water and mineral salts through a plant is the result of two forces, an upward push from the root system and an upward pull by the shoot system.

a Which process is responsible for the uptake of water by root systems, generating the upward push? (1 mark)

b Explain how transpiration generates the upward pull. (6 marks)

Revision Unit 6

Reproduction

The Check Up

1 Unicellular organisms reproduce asexually by simple cell division. What type of division is this? ____________

2 Name **two** organs used by plants as asexual reproductive structures.

____________ and ____________

3 Why are asexually produced populations more vulnerable to adverse changes in their environment than sexually produced populations? ____________

4 What is meant by the term 'fertilisation'? ____________

5 What does the term 'haploid' mean? ____________

6 Where are gametes formed in human i) males and ii) females? i) ____________ ii) ____________

7 Name the tube that links the human testis to the urethra. ____________

8 Which **three** glands produce the fluid part of semen?

____________ and ____________ and ____________

9 Name the tube that links the human ovary to the uterus. ____________

10 Where does fertilisation take place in the female human reproductive system? ____________

11 Name the nucleus formed by the fusion of gametes at fertilisation. ____________

12 What is the function of the anther of a stamen? ____________

13 Label **A–E** on the diagram.

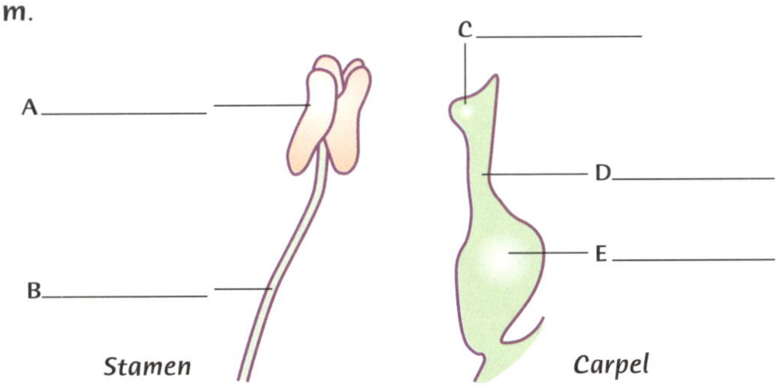

14 What is meant by the term 'pollination'? ____________

15 Name **two** agents employed by plants to carry out pollination.

____________ and ____________

16 State **one** difference between insect-pollinated and wind-pollinated flowers. ____________

17 How do male gametes get from the stigma to the inside of an ovule to fertilise the female gametes?

____

18 What does an ovule become after fertilisation? ____________

19 Which part of a flower is modified to form a fruit? ____________

20 What modification does a tomato fruit show to aid dispersal? ____________

Mark yourself *(see answers on page 109)*

- More than 12? Do the exam practice – or go on to another unit.
- Less than 12? Do the crash course on the next page.

/20

The Crash Course

Asexual reproduction

- Single-celled organisms reproduce asexually by **mitosis**.
- Some plants reproduce asexually by producing bulbs, corms, rhizomes or stem tubers.
- Asexually produced offspring have the same genes as their parents.

Sexual reproduction

- Sexual reproduction involves the production and fusion of dissimilar **gametes** or sex cells.
- This fusion of gametes is known as **fertilisation**.
  Fertilisation brings together two sets of chromosomes, one set from each gamete.
  This makes a **diploid** nucleus called a **zygote**.
- **Gametes** must be **haploid** (contain a single set of chromosomes) to maintain the diploid chromosome number for the species.
- The life cycle of a sexually reproducing organism must include a phase where **meiosis** occurs.

Remember:
- **Mitosis** produces daughter cells with the **same number** of chromosomes as their parent cell.
- **Meiosis halves the number** of chromosomes going into the daughter cells.

Human sexual reproduction

Human male reproductive organs

Side view

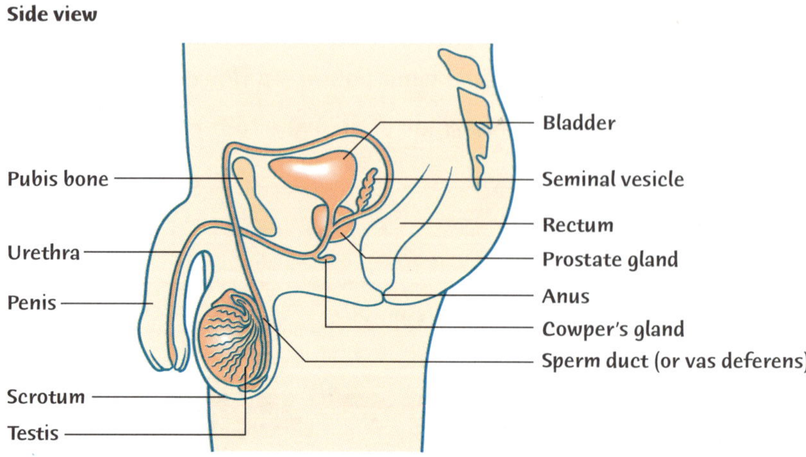

The Crash Course

Human female reproductive organs

Side view

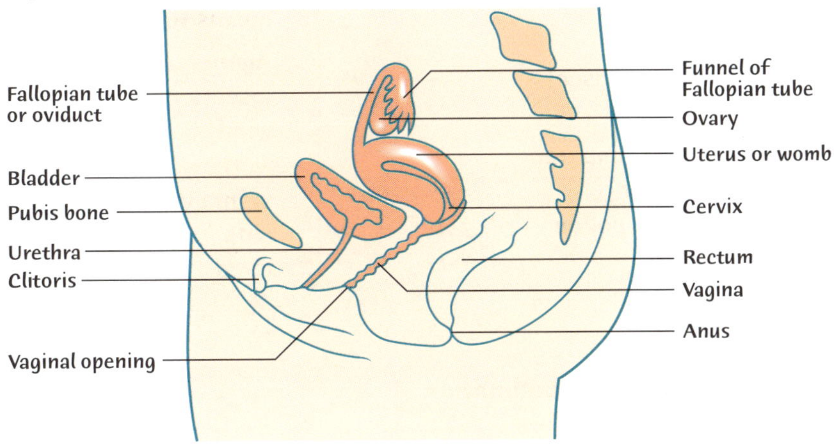

- **Sperms** are produced in the **testes**. **Eggs** are produced in the **ovaries**.
- **Fertilisation** takes place in the **oviduct** when a sperm and egg fuse.
- An **embryo** is the result of many cell divisions (mitosis).

Sexual reproduction in flowering plants

The sex organs of flowering plants are found in their **flowers**.

Sex organ	Function
Stamen	Produces pollen grains. The male gametes are inside the pollen grains
Carpel	Produces female gametes called egg cells. These are found deep inside the ovary of the carpel enclosed in a structure known as an ovule

The parts of a flower

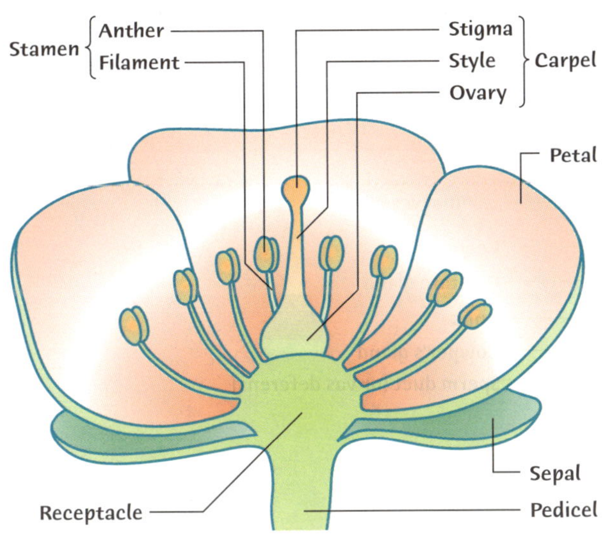

Continued

The Crash Course

Pollination involves the transfer of pollen from a stamen to a receptive stigma.

Plants have **flowers** that are **adapted to** their particular pollination **agent**.

Insect-pollinated flowers are large, and attractive to insects. They are coloured and produce nectar.

Wind-pollinated flowers are often inconspicuous. Compared to insect-pollinated flowers they have longer anther filaments, larger quantities of smaller aerodynamic pollen and exposed, net-like stigmas.

Remember:

Different plants use different means to get pollinated.

Agents used include:
insects
wind
water
monkeys
bats
birds

Events that take place in the flower after successful pollination:

1 pollen grain germinates
2 a pollen tube grows down, through the style
3 male nuclei pass through the pollen tube to enter the ovule
4 male nuclei fertilise female nuclei inside the ovule

After fertilisation:

1 an ovule becomes a seed
2 the wall of the ovary changes and the ovary becomes a fruit

Exam Practice

1 The diagrams show the human male and female reproductive organs in front view.

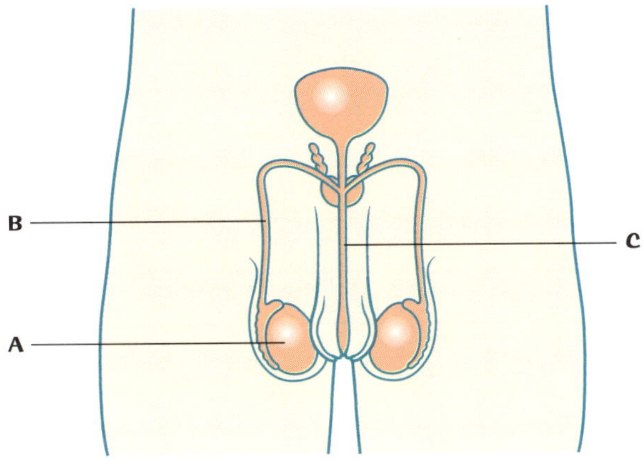

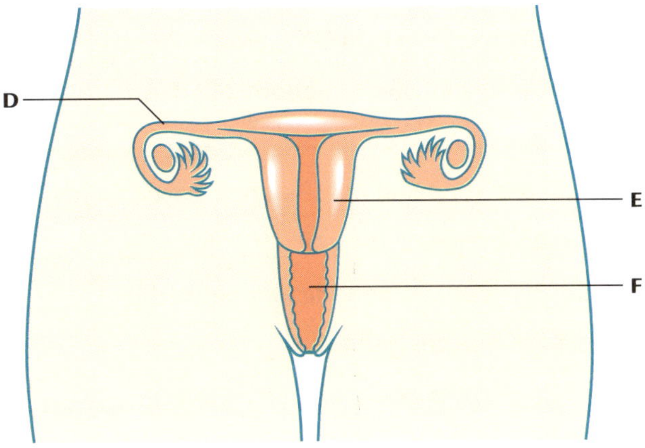

a Give labels for parts **A–F**. 6 marks

b State the letter of the part where sperms are produced. 1 mark

c State the letter of the part where fertilisation takes place. 1 mark

2 Write appropriate statements for **A–H** to complete the following table of features of an insect-pollinated flower and a wind-pollinated flower. 8 marks

	Insect-pollinated flower	Wind-pollinated flower
Petals	**A**	**B**
Stamens	**C**	**D**
Anthers	**E**	**F**
Stigmas	**G**	**H**

3 Describe the events that have to take place for an **insect**-pollinated flower to produce seeds successfully.

Your description should include reference to **pollination**, **fertilisation**, **seed** and **fruit development**. 9 marks

Revision Unit 1

Cell division, Variation, Inheritance and evolution

The Check Up

1 Chromosomes contain DNA. What special feature does DNA show? ______

2 What do we call short sections of DNA? ______

3 What does a gene code for? ______

4 What sort of chemical substance are enzymes made from? ______

5 What do enzymes do? ______

6 Basically, what do genetic engineers do? ______

7 What are mutant genes? ______

8 How do mutant genes arise naturally? ______

9 What is true about the genetics of daughter cells produced by mitosis? ______

10 How do the daughter cells of a single meiosis differ from their parent cell? ______

11 How does the chromosome number of a zygote differ from the chromosome number of each of the gametes involved in its formation? ______

12 Why does meiosis have to occur in a sexually reproducing organism? ______

13 Give **two** ways in which genetic variation can arise. ______

14 Which of the following is an example of continuous variation? Underline your choice.

Blood group   Gender   Height

15 Give the genotype for i) a human male and ii) a human female.

i)______   ii)______

16 What is an allele? ______

17 What is meant by the term 'homozygous'? ______

18 Complete the following checkerboard diagram:

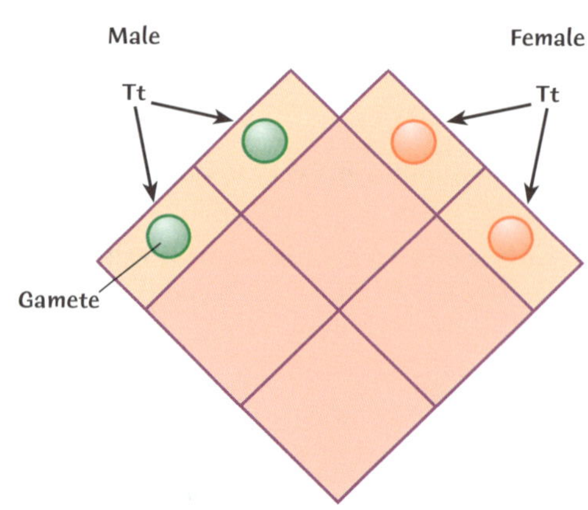

19 Name a sex-linked genetic disease. ______

20 What is meant by the term 'natural selection'? ______

Mark yourself *(see answers on page 110)*

- More than 12? Do the exam practice – or go on to another unit.
- Less than 12? Do the crash course on the next page.

/20

The Crash Course

Genes

DNA has a chemical structure that allows it to replicate (copy) itself. DNA occurs in chromosomes.

The way genes work:

1. Sections of DNA make up **genes**.
2. Each gene codes for the manufacture of a specific protein.
3. Enzymes are specific proteins that control specific biochemical reactions.
4. Specific biochemistry provides the potential for what an organism can do and be.

Changes in DNA will therefore change the enzymes produced and the chemistry they control. Therefore the outcome will change (variation). **Genetic engineering** uses this basic principle in introducing foreign genes into host DNA to make useful varieties.

Natural changes in DNA occur randomly. They are known as **mutations** and the genes are known as **mutant** genes. Mutations occur when mistakes are made in the copying of DNA that has to go on, when nuclei divide during cell division. Some chemicals and ionising radiation can increase the probability of random mutation. These agents are called **mutagens**.

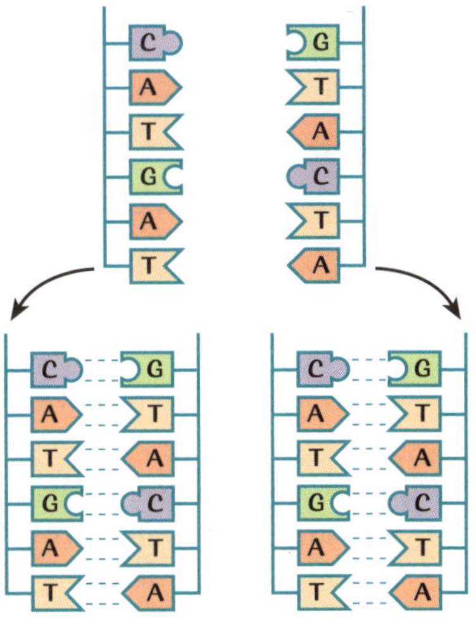

Replication of DNA

Symbol for radioactivity

Mitosis

The nucleus divides first:

1. The DNA of each chromosome in the dividing nucleus is **copied exactly** (replication).
2. One copy of each chromosome is moved to one of two separate places in the dividing cell.
3. Each group of copies is a new nucleus.

The cell then divides:

4. The cell membrane 'pinches-in', meets and separates the two nuclei, each with some cytoplasm.
5. Each daughter cell will contain, therefore, some cytoplasm and a nucleus with a copy of the same DNA as its parent.

Remember:

Mitosis produces **two identical daughter cells** diploid or haploid depending on the parent cell.

Human cell	Number of chromosomes	Description
Body cell, e.g. skin cell	46 (23 pairs)	Diploid
Sex cell, e.g. egg or sperm	23 (single)	Haploid

THE CRASH COURSE

Meiosis

Remember:

- A diploid nucleus contains two sets of chromosomes. One set came originally from the male gamete and the other from the egg. Every chromosome has a partner somewhere in the nucleus.
- Each pair is called a bivalent.

The nucleus divides first:

1 The individual members of each bivalent are separated each to a different place in the cell.
2 The collections of single chromosomes could form new nuclei at this point.
3 But, at the start of the division each chromosome had already replicated, so what appears to be a single chromosome is actually two copies held very closely together.
4 The copies are then separated into two places making four collections of single chromosomes.

Cell division then takes place:

5 **Four**, **haploid**, **sex cells** are formed by meiosis.

Variation

Variation in living things can result from genetic and environmental causes.

- **Continuous** variation results in a continuum between two extremes, e.g. height in humans.
- **Discontinuous** variation produces clear classes, such as blood group or gender.

Remember, genetic variation can occur:

- during meiosis;
- as a result of random fusion of gametes that takes place during fertilisation.

Inheritance

Single genes control some characteristics.

Term	Meaning
Allele	One form of a gene, e.g. **T** or **t**
Dominant allele	Always expressed, e.g. **TT** or **Tt**
Recessive allele	Only expressed when it is partnered by another like itself, e.g. **tt** or when it has no partner, e.g. when it is a sex-linked recessive
Homozygous	Two alleles of the same type for the same gene produce a homozygote, e.g. **TT** or **tt**
Heterozygote	Two different alleles for the same gene produce a heterozygote, e.g. **Tt**
Phenotype	The characteristic shown, e.g. tallness. The outcome of a particular genotype.
Genotype	The alleles present, e.g. a heterozygous tall plant would have the genotype, **Tt**

Continued ▶

The Crash Course

Gender is inherited by means of two chromosomes X and Y.
XX is female and **XY** is male.

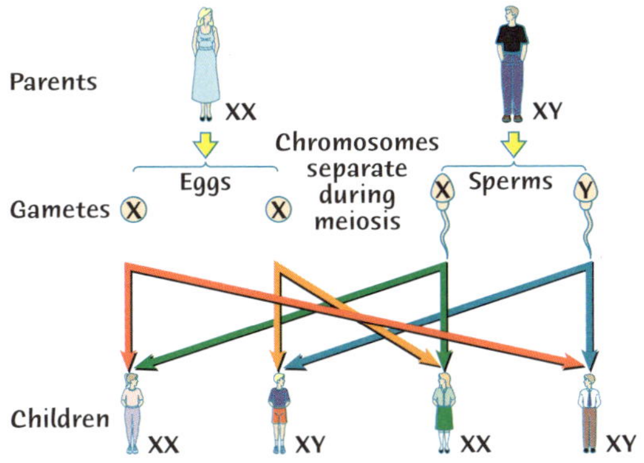

Inheritance of sex in humans

A cross between **two heterozygotes** gives potential offspring in the ratio of **3 : 1**.
A cross between a **heterozygote and a homozygous recessive** gives potential offspring in the ratio **1 : 1**.

Heterozygous × Heterozygous

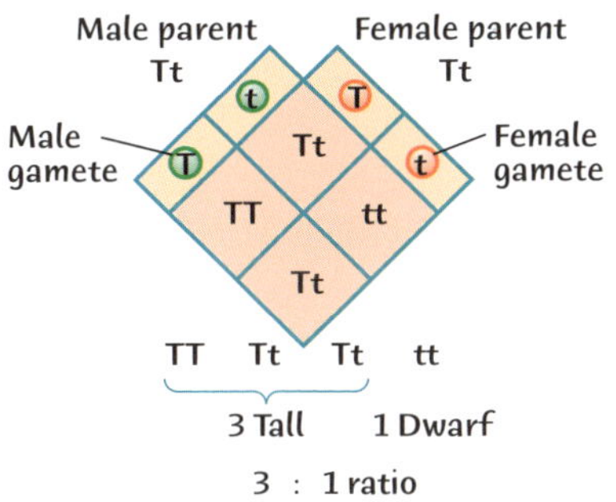

Heterozygous × Homozygous recessive

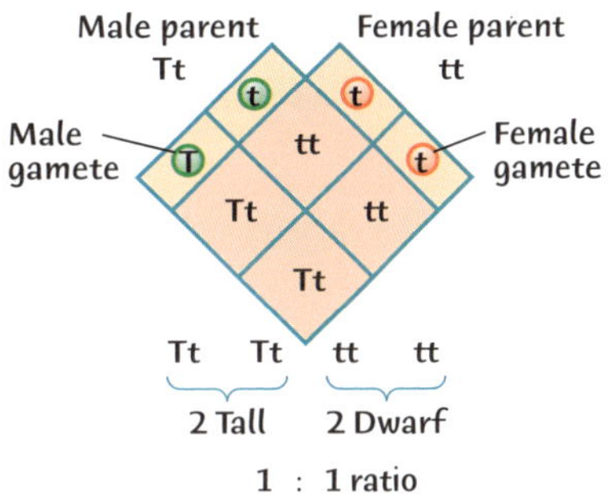

Remember:
- Some **disorders or diseases**, e.g. sickle-cell anaemia and cystic fibrosis, are caused by **recessive alleles**.
- Some diseases are **sex-linked**, e.g. muscular dystrophy and haemophilia. These are two examples caused by **X-linked recessive** alleles.

Evolution

Darwin proposed a hypothesis based on the concept of '**natural selection**' to explain evolution.

Key points:
1. Organisms over-reproduce.
2. Organisms compete for factors in their environment, e.g. food, space.
3. Some variants compete more successfully than others.
4. These survive and breed.
5. Their alleles are passed on to the next generation.

Advantageous variants may be selected by factors in the environment positively, leading to the survival and increasing frequency of certain alleles and, over time, to **evolutionary change**. Disadvantageous variants, having a negative effect, may become **extinct**.

Exam Practice

1 Explain how DNA controls the chemistry of a cell.
Use the following words in your answer:

chromosomes *enzymes* *genes* *metabolism* *proteins* — 4 marks

2 Distinguish between the following pairs of terms:

a gene and allele;

b dominant and recessive;

c gamete and zygote;

d homozygous and heterozygous. — 8 marks

3 The allele for black coat colour **B**, in guinea pigs is dominant to the allele for brown coat colour, **b**. Homozygous and heterozygous black guinea pigs are indistinguishable from each other.

a What are the genotypes for the following guinea pigs?

i) Pure breeding black

ii) Heterozygous black — 2 marks

b Which crosses would give:

i) a 3:1 ratio of black to brown, in the offspring, and

ii) a 1:1 ratio of black to brown, in the offspring? — 2 marks

c Which genotype would be the **most** useful for a guinea pig breeder to use in a breeding programme designed to sort out which black guinea pigs were homozygous and which were heterozygous?
Explain your answer. — 4 marks

4 Haemophilia is caused by an X-linked recessive.

The normal allele **H** is dominant to the recessive, **h**.

There is no allele on the Y chromosome.

The genotype for a normal male is $\mathbf{X_HY}$ and the genotype for a normal female is $\mathbf{X_HX_H}$.

The genotype for a haemophiliac male is $\mathbf{X_hY}$ and the genotype for a carrier female is $\mathbf{X_HX_h}$.

Consider the situation where a woman who is heterozygous for this condition intends to have children by a normal male.

a What name is given to someone who is heterozygous for a genetic disorder such as this? — 1 mark

b Draw a checkerboard diagram to explain what the probabilities of their children being normal or haemophiliac are. — 4 marks

Revision Unit 8

Ecosystems

The Check Up

1 Which group of organisms are called producers? ______

2 Which of the following feeding levels would be a herbivore?

producer ⟶ primary consumer ⟶ secondary consumer ______

3 How does a food web differ from a food chain? ______

4 Lions eat zebras. What names are given to the two species in this feeding relationship?

______

5 Some plants are adapted to avoid being eaten by animals. Give one example of such an adaptation.

______

6 Draw the typical shape of a 'pyramid of numbers' in the box.

7 What is 'biomass'? ______

8 Give **one** reason why the amount of biomass decreases at each step in a food chain.

______

9 What happens to most of the energy obtained by an organism from its food?

______

10 What part does photosynthesis play in the carbon cycle?

______

11 Name **two** processes that produce carbon dioxide from carbon compounds in the carbon cycle.

______ and ______

12 What do nitrifying bacteria in the soil do within the nitrogen cycle?

______

13 Which family of flowering plants is liable to infection by nitrogen-fixing bacteria? ______

14 Give one good reason for the use of pesticides. ______

15 Give one good reason for not using pesticides. ______

16 Why is much of the countryside in the UK described as an artificial ecosystem?

______

17 Name **three** fossil fuels. ______ ______ ______

18 Name **three** greenhouse gases. ______ ______ ______

19 Which gases dissolve in water in the atmosphere to produce acid rain? ______

20 Why is the loss of the world's rainforests a major cause for concern?

______

Mark yourself *(see answers on page 110)*

- More than 12? Do the exam practice – or go on to another unit.
- Less than 12? Do the crash course on the next page.

/20

THE CRASH COURSE

Food chains and food webs

Feeding level	Group	Diet
Producers	Plants	Make their own food by photosynthesis
Consumers	Herbivores	Eat plants
	Carnivores	Eat animals Some carnivores are called predators. The animals they eat are described as their prey
	Omnivores	Eat plants and animals

Producer (plant), e.g. oak tree ⟶ Primary consumer (herbivore), e.g. caterpillar ⟶ Secondary consumer (carnivore), e.g. blue tit ⟶ Tertiary consumer (carnivore), e.g. sparrowhawk

Food webs are used to represent a number of interrelated food chains.

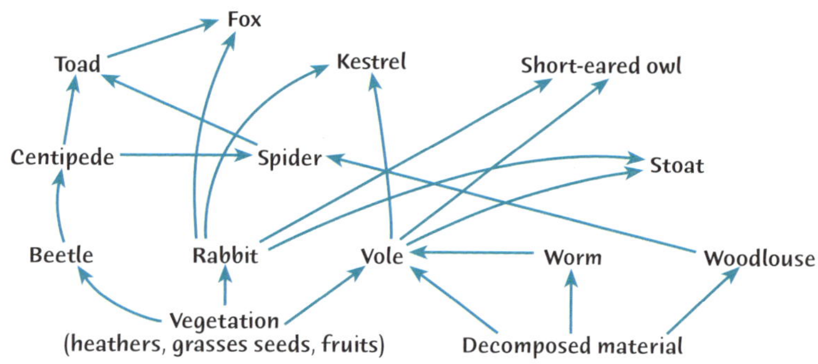

Food web for a moorland community

Plant and animal adaptations to feeding

Some plants show adaptations that enable them to reduce the risk of their being eaten by herbivores:

- low growth form, where their leaves are arranged as **rosettes**, close to the ground
- spines on stems or leaves
- stinging hairs
- poisonous or unpleasant-tasting chemicals in shoot tissues.

Predators have adaptations that enable them to **capture and kill** their food.
Prey animals show structural and behavioural adaptations, e.g. **herding** or the ability to run fast.

Pyramid of numbers, biomass and energy

Most food chains produce a 'number' graph that results in a pyramid shape – a **pyramid of numbers**.

The size of the individuals of the species involved however can affect the shape of the graph. A food chain where the producer is a single, large tree, e.g. an oak tree, will give a very small base to the pyramid, as shown on the next page.

THE CRASH COURSE

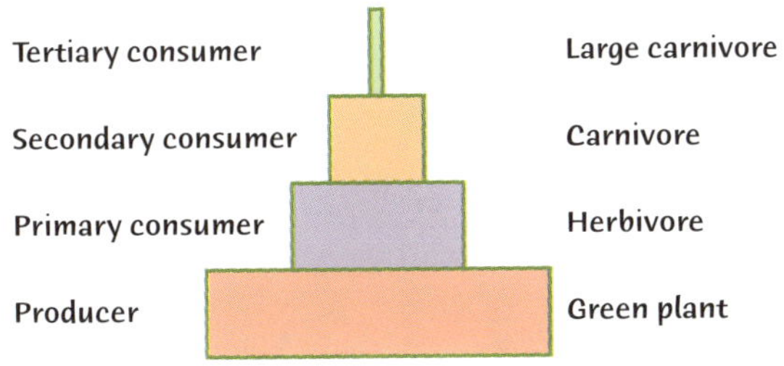

Standard pyramid of numbers

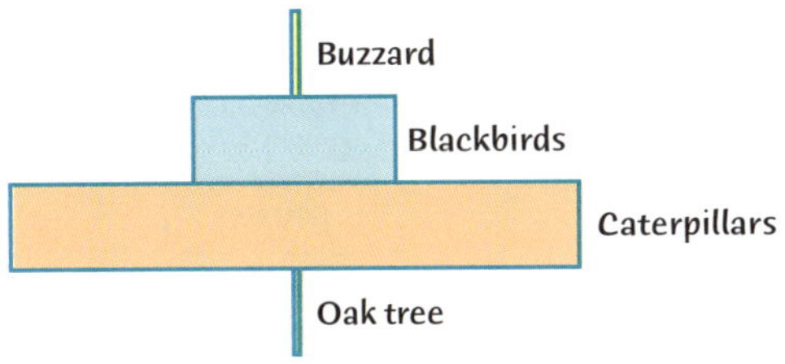

Oak tree pyramid

A **pyramid of biomass** will always have a larger base than the levels above it. Biomass is lost at each transfer due to factors such as:

- respiration
- loss by excretion
- indigestible material.

Much of the **energy** obtained by an organism by feeding is lost to the environment as heat and as a result of its use to keep the organism alive. Therefore less energy is transferred at each stage of a food chain. Energy transfer through the various feeding levels can also be represented graphically as a pyramid.

Cycling of elements – the carbon and nitrogen cycles

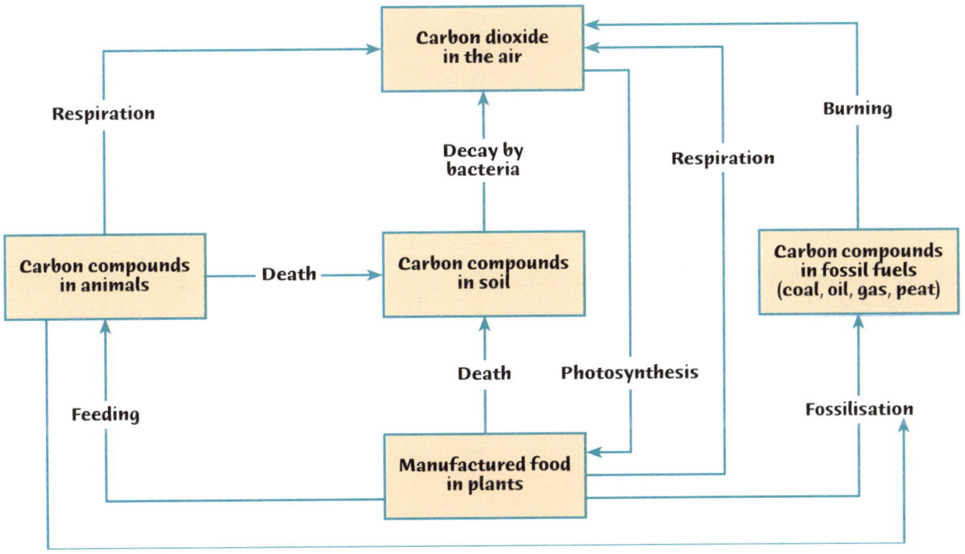

The carbon cycle

Continued ▶

The Crash Course

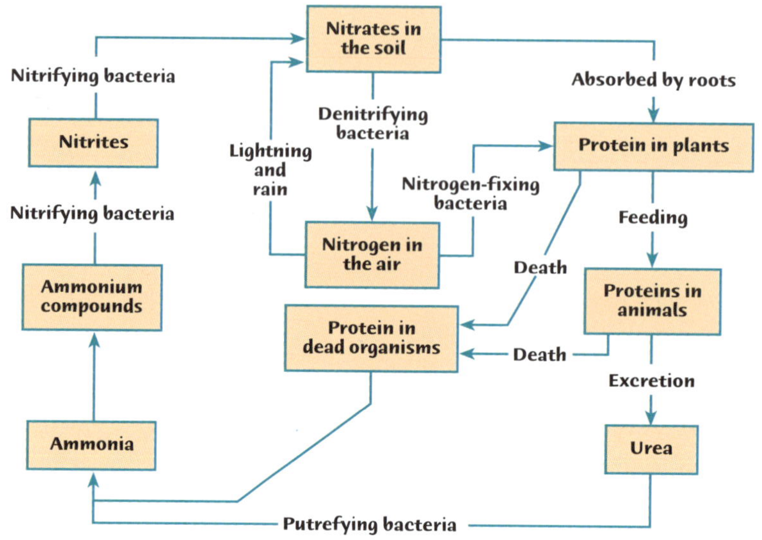

The nitrogen cycle

Humans and the environment

The world's increasing human population has numerous effects on the environment. Examples are:

1 destruction of natural ecosystems to build homes, factories etc.
2 creation of **artificial ecosystems** to produce food
3 use of **pesticides** at the production stage, and later when food is stored, to increase the yield of crop plants and animals (this often has a 'knock on' effect in natural food chains)
4 industry, agriculture and domestic activity worldwide generate a huge daily demand for energy.

Most of the world's energy needs are met, directly or indirectly, by the **burning of fossil fuels**.

Waste products released when fossil fuels are burnt:

Carbon dioxide
Sulphur dioxide
Nitrogen oxides

→

Consequences:

Acid rain
Greenhouse effect
Global warming

Rainforests have been reduced as a result of agricultural abuse or commercial resource stripping.

EXAM PRACTICE

1 The table includes brief descriptions of four organisms that live in the British countryside. They form a food chain that is part of a much more complex food web.

a In what way is a food web more complex than a food chain? 1 mark

Species		Nutrition
Accipiter nisus	(**A**)	Large, carnivorous bird
Helix aspersa	(**B**)	Small, herbivorous mollusc
Holcus lanatus	(**C**)	Photosynthetic
Turdus philomelos	(**D**)	Medium-sized, omnivorous bird, feeds principally on small invertebrates

Where appropriate use the capital letters **A–D** to answer the following questions.

b Which organism is a producer? 1 mark

c *Turdus philomelos* feeds on small invertebrates. What else must it eat if it is an omnivore? 1 mark

d Write a food chain to include organisms **A–D**. 3 marks

2 The numbers of organisms at each trophic level in a food chain can be represented graphically.

The diagram below shows two examples, **A** and **B**.

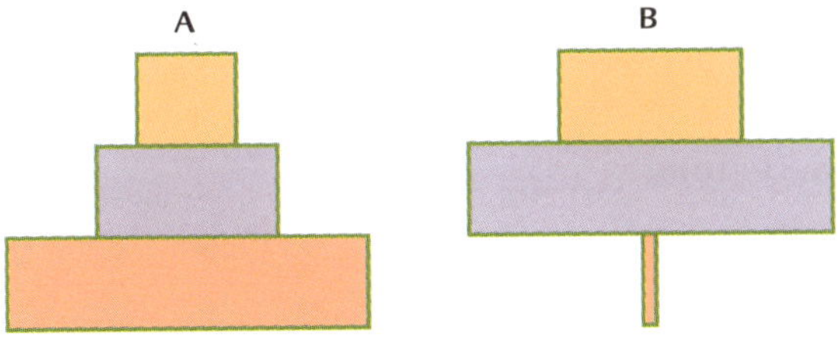

a What is the term used to describe graphs like **A** and **B**? 1 mark

b Explain the main difference between graph **B** and graph **A**. 2 marks

c i) What is meant by the term 'biomass'? 1 mark

ii) Draw outlines of the shape that would be obtained if biomass rather than number had been used to draw graphs **A** and **B**. 2 marks

3 a i) Which organisms are able to 'fix' carbon into carbon compounds using carbon dioxide as a source of 'free' carbon? 2 marks

ii) Name the first carbon compound made in this way. 1 mark

b Animals eat carbon compounds in their food.

Carbon compounds are used in a variety of ways by an animal.

How is the carbon released from the compounds to produce carbon dioxide:

i) while the animal is still alive, and

ii) after the animal has died and been buried? 4 marks

4 a What is meant by the term 'greenhouse effect'? Explain how the global increase in the combustion of fossil fuels has led to 'the greenhouse effect'. 3 marks

b Describe the consequences of the greenhouse effect for the world. 3 marks

Revision Unit 9

The structure of the atom

The Check Up

1 Put a ring around the name of the chemist who revived the idea of atoms in the early nineteenth century.

Boyle Bunsen Dalton Davy Priestley

2 What is an atom? ____________________

Complete the table showing some properties of protons, neutrons and electrons.

	Particle	Mass	Charge
	proton	1 amu	+1
3	neutron		
4	electron		

5 Which two particles are present in equal numbers in any atom? ____________ and ____________

6 How is a hydrogen-1 nucleus different from all other nuclei? ____________________

7 The nuclei of all atoms are positively charged. True or false? ____________

8 The diagram shows a lithium atom. Label the particles A, B and C on the diagram.

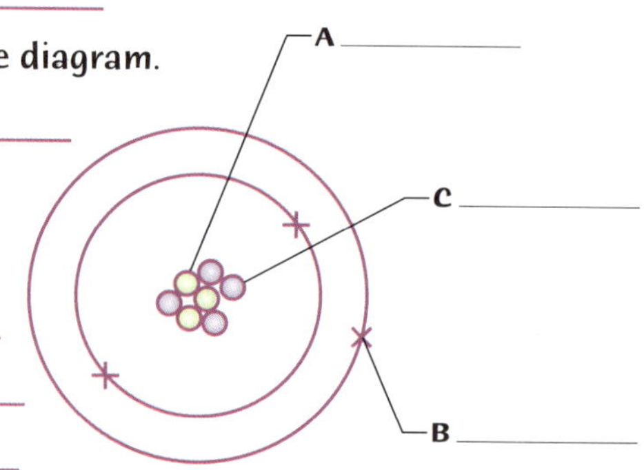

9 Where in the atom is the mass concentrated? ____________________

The symbol for a phosphorus-31 atom is shown here. $^{31}_{15}\mathrm{P}$

10 How many protons are there in a phosphorus-31 atom? ____________

11 How many electrons are there in a phosphorus-31 atom? ____________

12 How many neutrons are there in a phosphorus-31 atom? ____________

13 What is the atomic number of phosphorus? ____________

A sodium-23 atom contains 11 electrons.

14 How many nucleons are there in a sodium-23 atom? ____________

15 How many protons are there in a sodium-23 atom? ____________

16 What is the electron arrangement in a sodium-23 atom? ____________

17 What are isotopes? ____________________

____

18 Chlorine contains 75% chlorine-35 and 25% chlorine-37.

What is the relative atomic mass of chlorine? ____________

19 All isotopes are radioactive. True or false? ____________

20 Which particle, proton, neutron or electron, is lost or gained when an ion is formed? ____________

Mark yourself *(see answers on page 111)*

- More than 12? Do the exam practice – or go onto another unit.
- Less than 12? Do the crash course on the next page.

/ 20

THE CRASH COURSE

Structure of the atom

An **atom** is the smallest part of an element which can exist.

Atoms are made up of three types of particles.

particle	mass	charge
proton, p	1 unit	+1
electron, e	negligible	–1
neutron, n	1 unit	0

An atom contains equal numbers of protons and electrons and is therefore neutral.

Protons and neutrons are tightly packed together in the **nucleus**.

The electrons move around the nucleus in shells (or energy levels).

Each shell can hold up to a maximum number of electrons.

Two numbers can be used to describe any atom.

The **atomic number** of an atom is the number of protons in the nucleus.

The **mass number** of an atom is the number of nucleons (protons + neutrons) in the nucleus.

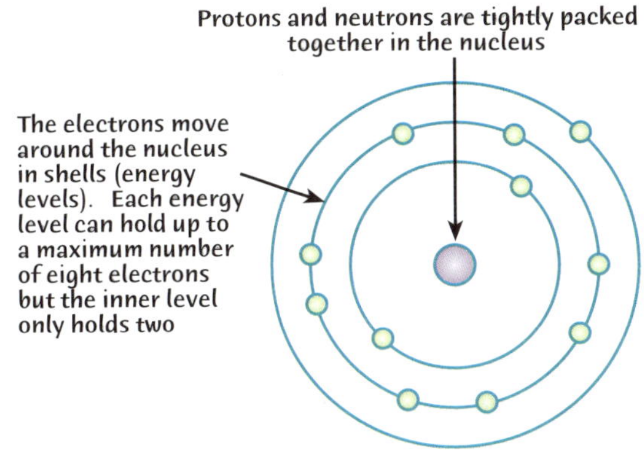

Electron configuration in a sodium atom

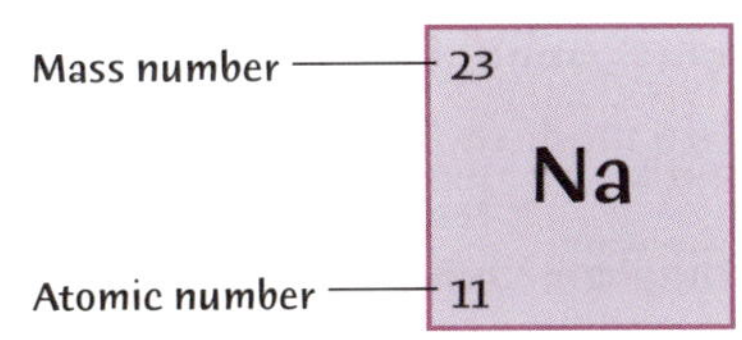

Isotopes

Atoms of the same element with different mass numbers are called isotopes.

Isotopes of the same element contain the same number of protons and electrons but different numbers of neutrons.

Relative atomic mass

The **relative atomic mass** (abbreviated to RAM or A_r) of an element is based upon the average mass of all the atoms in a sample of the element.

Any sample of chlorine is made up of 75% chlorine-35 and 25% chlorine-37. The relative atomic mass of chlorine is 35.5.

Many elements are composed of mixtures of different isotopes.

Isotopes are not always radioactive.

EXAMPLE

You work it out like this:

$$\frac{(75 \times 35) + (25 \times 37)}{100} = 35.5$$

Exam Practice

1 Draw diagrams showing the structure of atoms of carbon-12 and sodium-23. On each diagram label the protons, neutrons and electrons and include the number of each type of particle. You may look up carbon and sodium in the Periodic Table. 6 marks

2 Hydrogen exists as three isotopes, hydrogen-1, hydrogen-2 and hydrogen-3.

a In what ways are the structures of these three atoms similar and different? 2 marks

b How are the properties of these three isotopes similar and different? 2 marks

3 The element europium contains equal quantities of two isotopes, europium-151 and europium-153. The atomic number of europium is 63.

a How many protons, neutrons and electrons are there in each isotope? 4 marks

b What is the relative atomic mass of europium? 1 mark

4 John Dalton revived the idea of atoms.

He stated that

- all elements are made of atoms
- atoms cannot be split up into simpler particles.

How do modern ideas of atoms differ from those of Dalton? 4 marks

5 The diagram shows a sulphur-32 atom.

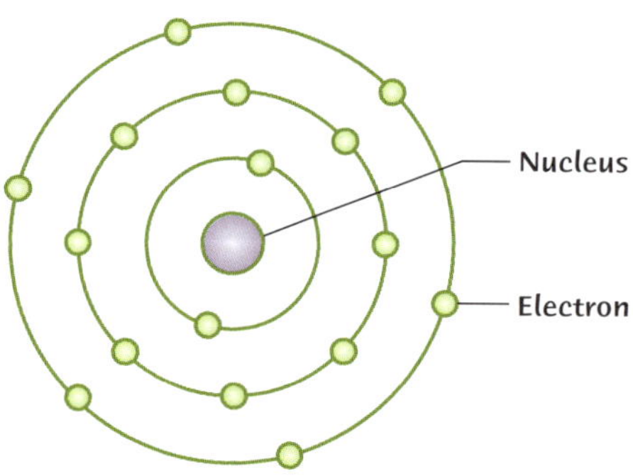

a How many protons, neutrons and electrons are there in a sulphur-32 atom? 3 marks

b What is the arrangement of electrons in a sulphur atom? 1 mark

c Look up oxygen in the Periodic Table. What is the arrangement of electrons in an oxygen atom? 1 mark

d What similarity is there in the arrangement of electrons in these two elements? 1 mark

Revision Unit 10

Particles, bonding and structure

The Check Up

1 Write down the names of two changes of state that require energy. ______________ and ______________

2 In which state of matter are particles most widely spaced? ______________

3 Which state of matter has a definite volume but takes up the shape of the bottom of the container?

____

4 The smell of perfume spreads throughout a room.

What name is given to the movement of particles to fill all of the available space? ______________

5 Of which type of bonding is sodium chloride the common example? ______________

6 What electronic change takes place when sodium combines with chlorine? ______________

7 Why does sodium chloride have a high melting point?

____

8 What name is given to a regular arrangement of ions in a sodium chloride crystal? ______________

The diagram shows a methane molecule.

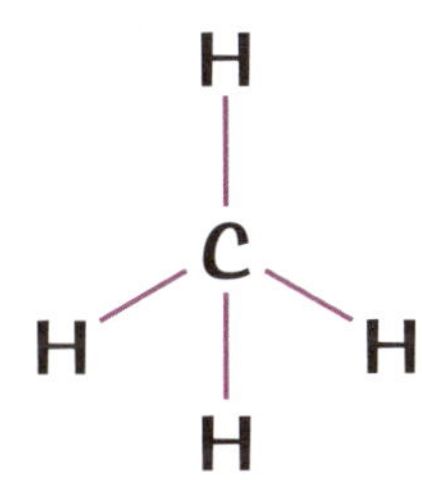

9 What type of bonding is present in a methane molecule?

____

10 What electronic change occurs when each bond is formed?

____

11 Why does methane have a very low melting and very low boiling point?

____

12 Two chlorine atoms join together to form a ______________ bond.

13 A chlorine atom contains 7 outer electrons. Finish the diagram to show the bonding in a chlorine molecule.

Cl Cl

14 Sodium chloride and silicon(IV) oxide are both giant structures. Sodium chloride is a giant structure of ______________ and silicon(IV) oxide of ______________ .

Magnesium oxide is another example of ionic bonding. A magnesium atom contains two outer electrons and an oxygen atom six outer electrons.

15 What change in electrons happens to a magnesium atom when it combines with oxygen?

____

16 What change in electrons happens to an oxygen atom when it combines with magnesium?

____

17 What ions are formed as a result of these changes? ______________

18 Why does magnesium oxide have a very high melting point? ______________

Continued ▶

The Check Up

19 Why is it wrong to refer to a magnesium oxide molecule? ______________________

20 Write down the names of two forms of carbon which have giant structures of atoms.

______________ and ______________

Mark yourself *(see answers on page 112)*

- More than 12? Do the exam practice – or go onto another unit.
- Less than 12? Do the crash course below.

/20

The Crash Course

Particles

Matter is made up of very tiny **particles**.

These particles may be individual atoms (e.g. helium) or groups of atoms called **molecules**.

These molecules may be made up of atoms of one element (e.g. in **elements** such as oxygen or sulphur) or more than one element (in **compounds** such as sodium chloride or ammonia).

States of matter

Matter can exist in three **states** (**solid**, **liquid** or **gas**) depending upon conditions of temperature and pressure.

This diagram shows a simple representation of particles in solids, liquids and gases.

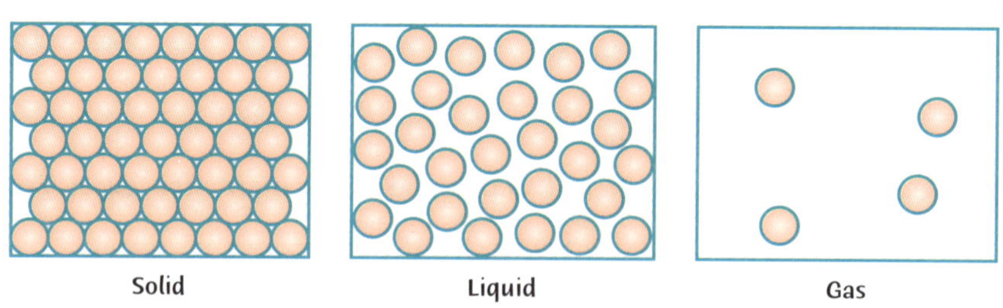

The particles in a solid are just vibrating. In a liquid the particles are moving more but it is only in a gas that particles move freely.

This diagram shows the changes between these three states of matter.

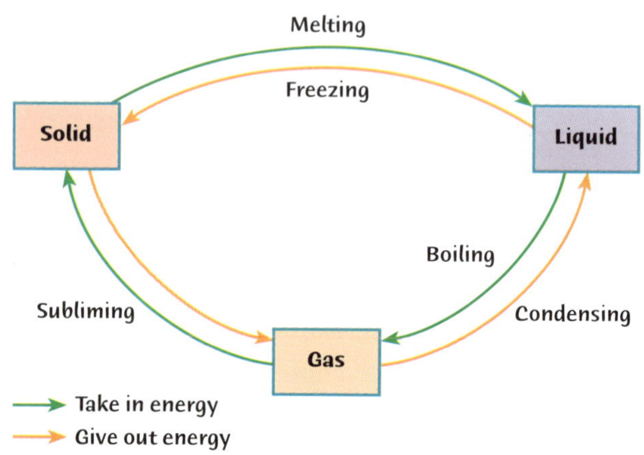

THE CRASH COURSE

Diffusion

Diffusion is the spreading of matter to fill all of the available space. This diagram shows the results of a diffusion experiment with bromine.

Diffusion takes place quicker in gases and extremely slowly in solids.

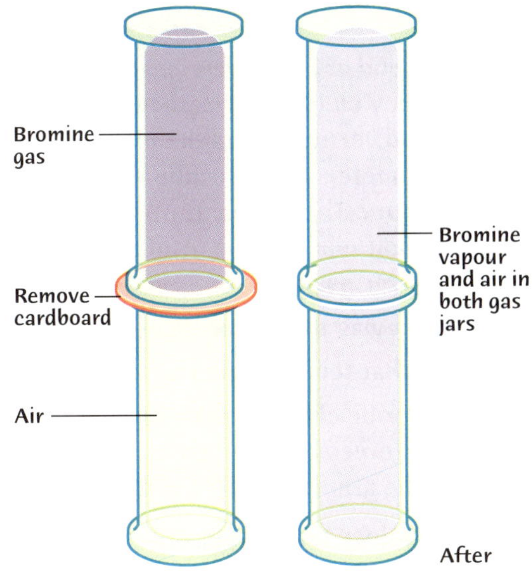

Diffusion in bromine

Bonding

Chemical bonds are forces which hold atoms together.

Two types of bond are the ionic bond and the covalent bond.

Ionic bonding, e.g. sodium chloride

A sodium atom has an electron arrangement of 2,8,1 and a chlorine atom has an electron arrangement of 2,8,7. Each sodium atom loses an electron and each chlorine atom gains an electron.

The resulting sodium Na^+ and chloride Cl^- ions are held together by strong electrostatic forces in a lattice (as shown here).

The strong forces between sodium and chloride ions result in a solid with a high melting point.

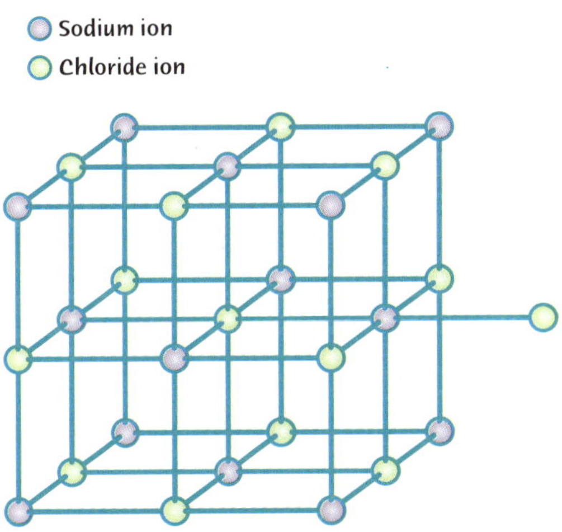

Structure of sodium chloride

Covalent bonding, e.g. hydrogen chloride

A covalent bond involves the sharing of a pair of electrons. In the case of hydrogen chloride, a hydrogen atom and a chlorine atom both provide an electron and this pair of electrons is used to hold the two atoms together.

Structure

When atoms are joined together they produce a structure.

Substances can have a **molecular structure**. This is made up of individual molecules with only very weak forces between molecules. An example is iodine.

Substances may have a **giant structure**. There are two types of giant structure:

- a giant structure of atoms, e.g. diamond, silicon(IV) oxide
- a giant structure of ions, e.g. sodium chloride.

Exam Practice

1 Some solid crystals were heated in a test-tube until they melted. The test-tube was then clamped vertically and the melt stirred with a thermometer. The test-tube was kept in the laboratory. The temperature was recorded every half minute. The results were displayed in a graph, as shown.

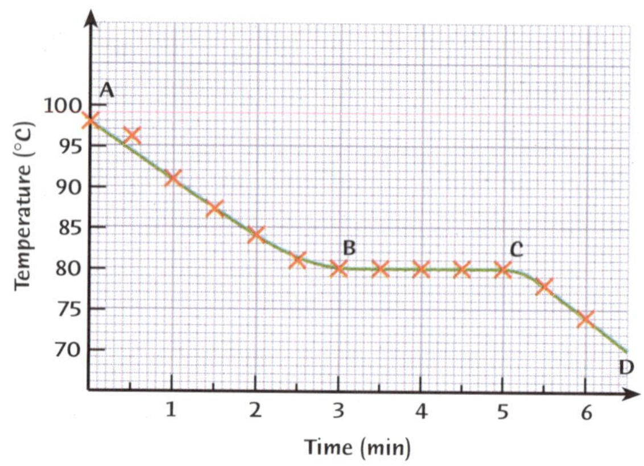

a What was the temperature after 2 min? **1 mark**

b At what temperature does the solid melt? **1 mark**

c Describe changes in movement of particles and forces between them in the three parts of the graph **AB**, **BC** and **CD**. **4 marks**

d Why does the temperature of the melt not fall between **B** and **C**? **1 mark**

2 A dry glass tube is clamped and pads of cotton wool soaked in ammonia solution and hydrogen chloride solution are put at opposite ends of the tube at the same time. After about 5 min a white ring forms, as shown.

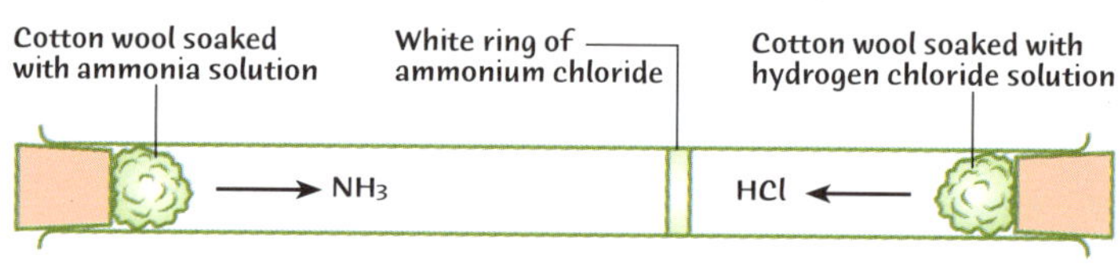

a Describe the position of the ring in the tube. **1 mark**

b What does the position of the ring tell you about the speed of movement of ammonia and hydrogen chloride particles? **2 marks**

c Suggest two reasons why the ring takes so long to form. **2 marks**

3 This diagram shows two forms of carbon – diamond and graphite.

a Explain why the structure of diamond makes it very hard. **1 mark**

b Explain why graphite is a good lubricant. **3 marks**

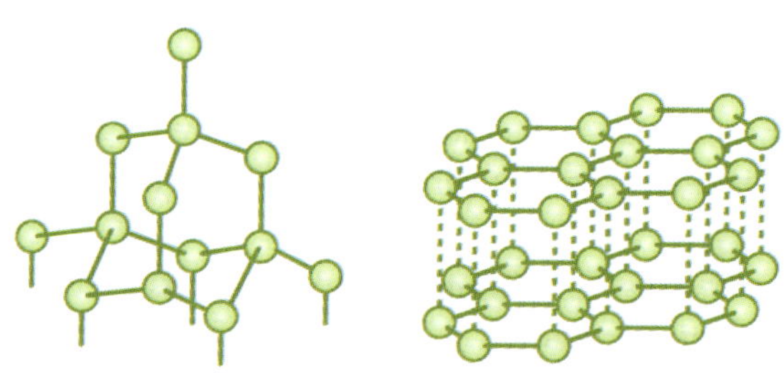

Diamond Graphite

4 a Dry hydrogen chloride is made up of molecules containing covalent bonding.

When hydrogen chloride dissolves in water a solution is produced which conducts electricity.

Explain the changes in bonding which take place. **2 marks**

b Sodium and hydrogen combine to form a solid called sodium hydride. Molten sodium hydride conducts electricity.

Describe the bonding in sodium hydride. **2 marks**

5 Magnesium oxide contains ionic bonding.

a Write down the electron arrangements of magnesium and oxygen atoms. **2 marks**

b Describe the changes in electron arrangement when magnesium and oxygen combine. **2 marks**

c Magnesium oxide has a melting point of 2827 °C and sodium chloride has a melting point of 801 °C. Why is the melting point of magnesium oxide so much greater than that of sodium chloride? **1 mark**

Revision Unit 11

Formulae, equations and calculations

The Check Up

DATA: Here is the data you will need to answer some of these questions. Relative atomic masses of elements: C = 12, N = 14, O = 16, Mg = 24, K = 39, Ca = 40, Fe =56, H = 1.
1 mol of any gas occupies 24 dm^3 at room temperature and atmospheric pressure (rtp).
Bond energies: H—H 436 kJ/mol, Cl—Cl 242 kJ/mol, H—Cl 431 kJ/mol

1 Which one of these symbols is not a symbol for a chemical element? M N O P ______________

2 Which one of these formulae is correct? KBr_2 CaOH NH_3 H_2NO_3 ______________

3 Write down the formula of aluminium oxide. ______________

4 Finish the symbol equation for the formation of water from oxygen and hydrogen.

$$H_2 + \quad O_2 \longrightarrow \quad H_2O$$

5 Calculate the relative formula mass (mass of 1 mol) of calcium carbonate, $CaCO_3$. ______________

6 The equation for the burning of magnesium in oxygen is $2Mg + O_2 \longrightarrow 2MgO$

What mass of magnesium oxide is produced from 48 g of magnesium? ______________

7 What state symbols are used for ice, liquid water and steam? ______________

8 What volume does 2 g of hydrogen, H_2, occupy at rtp? ______________

Here is a list of the formulae of oxides of nitrogen: NO N_2O NO_2 N_2O_4 N_2O_5

9 Which of these oxides has a relative formula mass (mass of 1 mol) of 30? ______________

10 Which of these nitrogen oxides contains the greatest percentage of nitrogen? ______________

11 Balance the equation: $NH_3 + \quad O_2 \longrightarrow \quad NO + \quad H_2O$

12 $2NO(g) + O_2(g) \rightleftharpoons 2NO_2(g)$

What is the meaning of the sign $\rightleftharpoons$ in this equation? ______________

The equation for the action of heat on potassium hydrogencarbonate is:

$$2KHCO_3(s) \longrightarrow K_2CO_3(s) + H_2O(l) + CO_2(g)$$

13 What mass of potassium carbonate can be produced from 10 g of potassium hydrogencarbonate?

____

14 What volume of CO_2, at rtp, can be produced from 10 g of potassium hydrogencarbonate?

____

15 Potassium hydrogencarbonate reacts with dilute sulphuric acid, H_2SO_4, to produce potassium sulphate, water and carbon dioxide. Write a balanced symbol equation for this reaction.

____

16 What mass of iron could be extracted from 160 g of pure iron(III) oxide, Fe_2O_3? ______________

The reaction of hydrogen and chlorine can be represented by

$$H—H + Cl—Cl \longrightarrow H—Cl + H—Cl$$

17 Calculate the energy change when 1 mol of hydrogen and 1 mol of chlorine react together.

____

Continued ▶

The Check Up

18 Is this reaction exothermic or endothermic? Explain your answer.

___

19 What mass of potassium hydroxide is needed to make 1 dm^3 of potassium hydroxide solution of concentration 2 mol/dm^3? ___

20 $2KOH + H_2SO_4 \longrightarrow K_2SO_4 + 2H_2O$

How many moles of potassium hydroxide are needed to react with 1 mol of sulphuric acid? ___

Mark yourself *(see answers on page 112)*

- More than 12? Do the exam practice – or go onto another unit
- Less than 12? Do the crash course below.

/20

The Crash Course

Chemical symbols and formulae

Each chemical element is represented by one or two letters called a **symbol**. The first letter is capital. Examples include carbon C, oxygen O, magnesium Mg and sodium Na. You can get the correct symbol for an element from the Periodic Table.

Each compound can be represented by a **formula**.

The formula gives the number of atoms of each element combined together. For example the formula for water is H_2O. In each molecule of water, two hydrogen atoms are combined with one oxygen atom.

Chemical equations

A **word equation** is a summary in words of a chemical reaction.

A **balanced symbol equation** uses correct chemical symbols to summarise a reaction, e.g. $CaCO_3(s) + 2HCl(aq) \longrightarrow CaCl_2(aq) + H_2O(l) + CO_2(g)$

In a **balanced equation** the number of atoms of **reactants** on the left-hand side must equal the number of atoms of **products** on the right-hand side.

A sign $\longrightarrow$ shows the direction of the reaction.The sign $\rightleftharpoons$ means that the reaction is reversible.

State symbols are: (s) – solid, (aq) – aqueous solution, (l) – liquid, (g) – gas. These do not have to be given unless they are asked for.

In an **ionic equation** the sum of the charges on the left-hand side is the same as the sum of the charges on the right-hand side.

Relative atomic mass

The **relative atomic mass** (A_r) is the number of times an atom of the element is heavier than a hydrogen atom.

Example

Carbon, (A_r =12) .

A carbon atom is 12 times heavier than a hydrogen atom.

THE CRASH COURSE

Relative formula mass (mass of 1 mol)

The relative formula mass M_r of a compound can be found from its formula by adding the masses of all the atoms in it.

The formula mass in grams of any substance contains the same large number of particles, namely 6×10^{23} or 600 000 000 000 000 000 000 000.

1 mol of any gas occupies 24 dm^3 at room temperature and atmospheric pressure (rtp).

A solution of concentration 1 mol/dm^3 contains 1 mol of solute dissolved in 1 dm^3 or 1000 cm^3 of solution.

EXAMPLE

H_2O $M_r = 1 + 1 + 16 = 18$

Finding chemical formula

The chemical formula of a compound can be found by experiment. The ratio of the atoms combining can be found by dividing the mass reacting by the appropriate A_r.

Calculations from equations

A balanced symbol equation can be used to calculate the masses of products and reactants needed.

Bond energy calculations

Energy is needed to break bonds and energy is released when bonds form.

The **bond energy** is the energy required to break 1 mol of bonds.

The difference between the energy required to break bonds and the energy released when bonds form is the overall energy change.

In an **exothermic** reaction the overall energy change is **negative** and in an **endothermic** reaction the energy change is **positive**.

In **exothermic** reactions heat is **given out** as the temperature rises.

In **endothermic** reactions heat is **taken in** as the temperature falls.

EXAM PRACTICE

1 Some of the following symbol equations are incorrect. Write out each incorrect equation correctly.

a $Al(s) + HCl(aq) \longrightarrow AlCl_3(aq) + H(g)$

b $O^{2-}(s) + H^+(aq) \longrightarrow H_2O(l)$

c $MgO(s) + 2HNO_3(aq) \longrightarrow Mg(NO_3)_2(aq) + H_2O(l)$

d $Mg(s) + 2HCl(aq) \longrightarrow MgCl_2(aq) + H_2(g)$

e $2K(s) + 2H_2O(l) \longrightarrow K(OH)_2(aq) + 2H(g)$

f $CaCO_3(s) + H_2O(l) + CO_2(g) \longrightarrow CaHCO_3(aq)$ **4 marks**

EXAM PRACTICE

2 Here is a list of common ions. You can use them to work out the formulae of compounds.

Cations (positively charged)		Anions (negatively charged)	
sodium	Na^+	chloride	Cl^-
potassium	K^+	bromide	Br^-
ammonium	NH_4^+	iodide	I^-
silver	Ag^+	hydroxide	OH^-
copper	Cu^{2+}	nitrate	NO_3^-
lead	Pb^{2+}	hydrogencarbonate	HCO_3^-
magnesium	Mg^{2+}	sulphate	SO_4^{2-}

Cations (positively charged)		Anions (negatively charged)	
calcium	Ca^{2+}	carbonate	CO_3^{2-}
zinc	Zn^{2+}	oxide	O^{2-}
barium	Ba^{2+}	sulphide	S^{2-}
iron(II)	Fe^{2+}	phosphate	PO_4^{3-}
iron(III)	Fe^{3+}		
aluminium	Al^{3+}		

For example, magnesium chloride is made up from Mg^{2+} and Cl^-. In the compound the overall charge must be zero and the formula is written as $MgCl_2$ (i.e. one magnesium ion and two chloride ions).

Write down the simplest formulae for: a potassium chloride; b zinc oxide; c zinc carbonate; d zinc hydroxide; e aluminium hydroxide; f aluminium phosphate; g ammonium chloride; h ammonium sulphate; i ammonium hydrogencarbonate; j iron(III) sulphate

5 marks

3 To find the formula of magnesium oxide, a weighed amount of magnesium ribbon is burnt in a crucible (as shown).

The results of an experiment are:

Mass of crucible and lid = 25.15 g

Mass of crucible and lid and magnesium = 25.27 g

Mass of crucible and lid and magnesium oxide = 25.35 g

Use this data to show that the formula of magnesium oxide is MgO. (Relative atomic masses: Mg = 24, O = 16)

4 marks

4 4.14 g of lead combines with oxygen to form 4.78 g of lead oxide. Calculate the simplest formula for this lead oxide. (Relative atomic masses: Pb = 207, O=16)

4 marks

5 The equation for the reaction between calcium carbonate and hydrochloric acid is:

$$CaCO_3(s) + 2HCl(aq) \longrightarrow CaCl_2(aq) + H_2O(l) + CO_2(g)$$

(Relative atomic masses: Ca = 40, C = 12, O = 16, H = 1, Cl = 35.5)

A sample of calcium carbonate with mass 10 g reacts with excess hydrochloric acid.

a Calculate the mass of calcium chloride formed.

3 marks

b Calculate the volume of carbon dioxide formed at room temperature and pressure.

2 marks

6 The equation for the Haber Process is

$$N_2 + 3H_2 \rightleftharpoons 2NH_3$$

The bond energies are N≡N 944 kJ/mol; H—H 436 kJ/mol; N—H 388 kJ/mol

Calculate the overall energy change when one mole of nitrogen (N_2) is converted into ammonia.

3 marks

Revision Unit 12

The Periodic Table

The Check Up

Here is a copy of the main parts of the modern Periodic Table.

Period	Group 1	Group 2											Group 3	Group 4	Group 5	Group 6	Group 7	Group 0
1						1 H Hydrogen 1												4 He Helium 2
2	7 Li Lithium 3	9 Be Beryllium 4											11 B Boron 5	12 C Carbon 6	14 N Nitrogen 7	16 O Oxygen 8	19 F Fluorine 9	20 Ne Neon 10
3	23 Na Sodium 11	24 Mg Magnesium 12	*d-block* transition elements										27 Al Aluminium 13	28 Si Silicon 14	31 P Phosphorus 15	32 S Sulphur 16	35.5 Cl Chlorine 17	40 Ar Argon 18
4	39 K Potassium 19	40 Ca Calcium 20	45 Sc Scandium 21	48 Ti Titanium 22	51 V Vanadium 23	52 Cr Chromium 24	55 Mn Manganese 25	56 Fe Iron 26	59 Co Cobalt 27	59 Ni Nickel 28	64 Cu Copper 29	65 Zn Zinc 30	70 Ga Gallium 31	73 Ge Germanium 32	75 As Arsenic 33	79 Se Selenium 34	80 Br Bromine 35	84 Kr Krypton 36
5	85.5 Rb Rubidium 37	88 Sr Strontium 38	89 Y Yttrium 39	91 Zr Zirconium 40	93 Nb Niobium 41	96 Mo Molybdenum 42	99 Tc Technetium 43	101 Ru Ruthenium 44	103 Rh Rhodium 45	106 Pd Palladium 46	108 Ag Silver 47	112 Cd Cadmium 48	115 In Indium 49	119 Sn Tin 50	122 Sb Antimony 51	128 Te Tellurium 52	127 I Iodine 53	131 Xe Xenon 54
6	133 Cs Caesium 55	137 Ba Barium 56	139 La Lanthanum 57	178.5 Hf Hafnium 72	181 Ta Tantalum 73	184 W Tungsten 74	186 Re Rhenium 75	190 Os Osmium 76	192 Ir Iridium 77	195 Pt Platinum 78	197 Au Gold 79	201 Hg Mercury 80	204 Tl Thallium 81	207 Pb Lead 82	209 Bi Bismuth 83	210 Po Polonium 84	210 At Astatine 85	222 Rn Radon 86
7	223 Fr Francium 87	226 Ra Radium 88	227 Ac Actinium 89	– Db Dubnium 104	– Jl Joliotium 105	– Rf Rutherfordium 106	– Bh Bohrium 107	– Hn Hassium 108	– Mt Meitnerium 109									

1 What name is given to a horizontal row in the Periodic Table? ______________________________

2 What name is given to a vertical column in the Periodic Table? ______________________________

3 Put a ring around the name of the man credited with producing the first Periodic Table.

Boyle **Dalton** **Davy** **Mendeleev** **Rutherford**

4 Which family of elements were not known when the Periodic Table was devised and now make up group 0?

____

5 The elements in the **original** Periodic Table were arranged in order of increasing ______________________________.

6 The elements in the **modern** Periodic Table are arranged in order of increasing ______________________________.

7 The elements in group 1 are in a family called the ______________________________.

8 The least reactive element in group 1 is ______________________________.

9 The elements in group 7 of the Periodic Table are in a family called the ______________________________.

10 The most reactive element in group 7 is ______________________________.

11 The block of elements between groups 2 and 3 is called the ______________________________.

12 The zig-zag line in bold on the table divides ______________ on the left-hand side from ______________ on the right.

13 Where in the Periodic Table are all the elements found that are gases at room temperature and atmospheric pressure? ______________________________

14 Put a ring around the element in the list below in group 3 of the Periodic Table.

aluminium **carbon** **phosphorus** **sodium**

15 Put a ring around the element in the list below in period 1 of the Periodic Table.

fluorine **helium** **nitrogen** **oxygen** **sodium**

16 Which is the first element in the Periodic Table? ______________________________

Continued ▶

THE CHECK UP

17 Which element has atoms containing three protons and three electrons? ______________________

18 The element with atomic number 32 was not known when the Periodic Table was devised but was found later. Write down the name of this element. ______________________

19 In any group of the Periodic Table the radius of the atoms (decreases/increases) down the group. ______________________

20 In any period of the Periodic Table the radius of atoms (decreases/increases) across the period from left to right. ______________________

Mark yourself *(see answers on page 113)*

- More than 12? Do the exam practice – or go onto another unit.
- Less than 12? Do the crash course below.

/20

THE CRASH COURSE

The Periodic Table is an arrangement of the elements in order of increasing **atomic number** such that elements with similar properties are in the same vertical group.
It was first devised by Mendeleev in 1869. In his table he arranged the elements in order of increasing atomic mass. However, in this way some elements were out of place.

Structure of the Periodic Table

Horizontal rows are called **periods** and vertical columns are called **groups**.
The bold zig-zag line divides **metals** on the left-hand side from **non-metals** on the right.
The elements between groups 2 and 3 make up the **transition metals**. These are relatively dense metals such as iron and nickel.
Transition metals form coloured compounds, e.g. copper(II) sulphate or chromium(III) sulphate.
Transition metals and their compounds often act as **catalysts**. This is because they can form different ions, e.g. iron can form Fe^{2+} and Fe^{3+} ions.
Atoms of an element in the main block (groups 1 to 0) contain the same number of electrons in the outer shell as the group the element is in. The exception to this is the noble gases in group 0 which have full outer shells. Helium has two outer electrons and the other elements in group 0 each have eight.

The Crash Course

Alkali metals

The family of metals in group 1 are called **alkali metals**.

Alkali metals are reactive metals stored under paraffin oil.

They react with cold water to form hydrogen gas and a hydroxide which is an alkali.

$2Na + 2H_2O \longrightarrow 2NaOH + H_2$

The reactivity of alkali metals increases down the group.

Halogens

The family of non-metals in group 7 is called **halogens**.

Fluorine and chlorine are gases, bromine is a liquid and iodine is a solid at room temperature and pressure.

All halogen molecules exist as pairs of atoms, e.g. Cl_2.

The halogens decrease in reactivity down the group.

The difference in reactivity can be shown by **displacement reactions**.

This reaction occurs because chlorine is more reactive than bromine.

Example

An example of a displacement reaction is the reaction between chlorine and potassium bromide.

$2KBr + Cl_2 \longrightarrow 2KCl + Br_2$

Changes in atomic radius

In any group the atoms of the elements become larger down the group. This is because one additional shell is added each time.

In a period the atoms become smaller across the period from left to right. This is despite the fact that additional protons, neutrons and electrons are added. The electrons are added to the same electron shell and there is more attraction between the nucleus and the outer electrons making the atom smaller.

Exam Practice

1 The table gives some information about three elements in Group 1.

element	atomic number	melting point (°C)	boiling point (°C)
lithium	3	181	1331
sodium	11	98	890
potassium	19	63	766

a What pattern is there in the melting and boiling points of these three elements? (2 marks)

b Rubidium is the next element in the group. Predict the melting point and boiling point of rubidium. (2 marks)

c Describe what you **see** when potassium reacts with cold water. (3 marks)

d Explain why the reactivity of metals in group 1 increases down the group. Use your ideas of atomic structure in your answer. (3 marks)

2 Elements in group 7 include chlorine, bromine and iodine.

a When chlorine gas is bubbled through potassium iodide the solution changes colour.

i) What colour change would you see? (2 marks)

ii) Write a balanced symbol equation for the reaction taking place. (2 marks)

b A mixture of hydrogen and chlorine reacts explosively to form a single product.

i) What is the name of this product? (1 mark)

ii) Write a balanced symbol equation for this reaction. (2 marks)

c Xenon is a noble gas. In 1963 chemists found that it would react with one of the halogen elements.

i) Which one of these elements reacted with xenon and why do you think it is this one? (2 marks)

ii) Why was this discovery unexpected? (1 mark)

3 In Mendeleev's original Periodic Table elements were arranged in order of increasing atomic mass. If we do this some elements are out of order.

a Write down the name of a pair of elements that are out of order when elements are arranged in order of increasing atomic mass. (1 mark)

b Show how arranging these elements in a modern Periodic Table puts them in the correct order. (2 marks)

c Explain why this pair of elements was out of order. Use your knowledge of atomic structure in your answer. (2 marks)

Revision Unit 13

Chemistry of carbon compounds

The Check Up

1 What are hydrocarbons? __________

2 Alkanes are saturated hydrocarbons. What is the meaning of the word saturated?

____

3 Put a ring around the formulae of the alkanes in this list.

C_2H_6 C_3H_6 C_8H_{18} C_6H_6

4 What is the name and formula of the simplest alkane? __________

5 In what raw material are alkanes found? __________

6 How are alkanes obtained from this raw material? __________

7 Put a ring around the hydrocarbon fraction that has the lowest boiling point.

lubricating oil paraffin petrol

8 What is the molecular formula of propane? __________

9 What are the products of combustion of an alkane in excess air?

____

10 What are the products of combustion of an alkane in limited air?

____

11 What is the name of the process used to break up long chain alkanes into short molecules?

____

12 What are these short molecules used for? __________

13 What is the name and formula of the simplest alkene? __________

14 What is present in the structure of all alkenes but is not present in the structure of alkanes? __________

15 What colour change is seen when ethene is bubbled through a solution of bromine? __________

16 What is the compound formed when ethene is bubbled through a solution of bromine? __________

17 What is the name given to compounds with the same molecular formula but different structural formulae? __________

18 Sugar is a carbohydrate. What is meant by the term carbohydrate?

____

19 What carbon compounds are formed when enzymes in yeast act on sugar solution?

____

20 What is the name of the process in question 19?

____

Mark yourself *(see answers on page 114)*

- More than 12? Do the exam practice – or go onto another unit.
- Less than 12? Do the crash course on the next page.

/20

The Crash Course

Hydrocarbons

Hydrocarbons are compounds of carbon and hydrogen **only**. There are different families (or **homologous series**) of hydrocarbons.

Alkanes

Alkanes are compounds with a general formula C_nH_{2n+2}.

Alkanes contain only single covalent bonds and are said to be **saturated**.

The simplest alkane is methane, CH_4.

Other common alkanes are ethane, C_2H_6, and propane, C_3H_8.

Butane has the formula C_4H_{10}. It can exist in two different structures or **isomers**, as shown.

Alkanes are found in a complicated mixture in crude oil (petroleum).

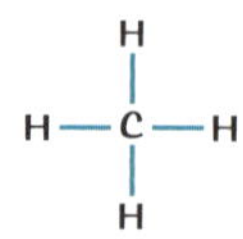
Methane

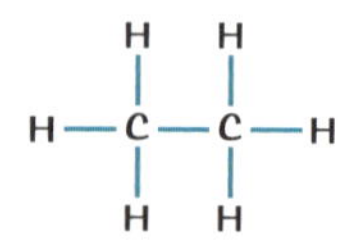
Ethane

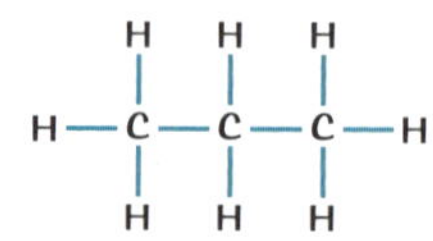
Propane

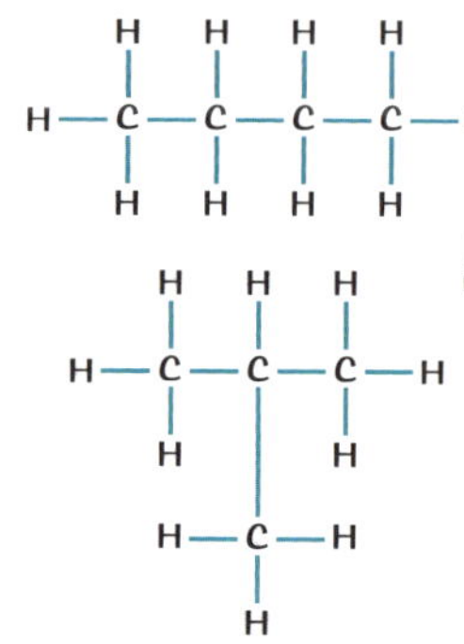
Butane isomers

Crude oil

Crude oil was formed millions of years ago by the action of high temperatures and high pressures on deposited dead sea creatures in the absence of air.

Crude oil is found underground trapped between layers of rock (see diagram).

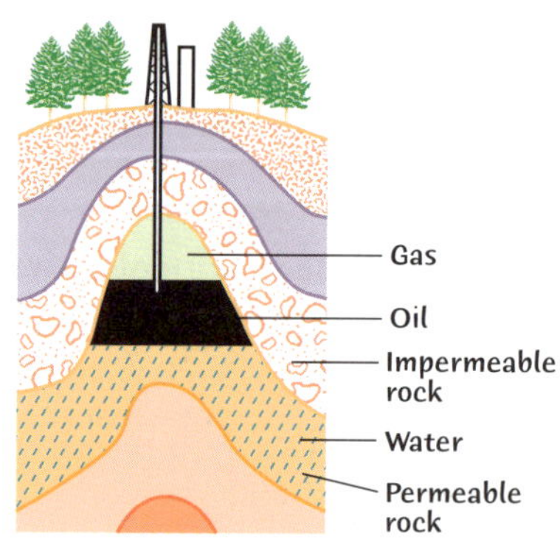

Fractional distillation

Crude oil is separated into saleable products by fractional distillation in a fractionating column (as shown). This separates compounds according to differences in boiling point.

Low boiling point fractions, such as petrol, condense high in the column and high boiling point fractions, such as lubricating oil, separate low in the column.

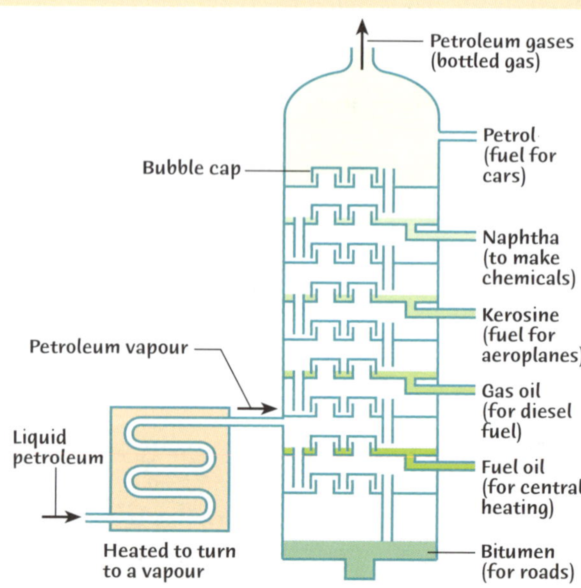

THE CRASH COURSE

Alkanes as fuels

Alkanes burn in air or oxygen and are often used as **fuels**.

Burning an alkane in excess air produces **carbon dioxide** and **water**.

Burning an alkane in a limited supply of air produces **carbon monoxide** and **water**. Carbon monoxide is very poisonous.

Cracking

Higher boiling point fractions which are not easy to sell can be broken down into small unsaturated molecules by the process of **cracking**.

Cracking requires high temperatures and a catalyst.

Alkenes

Alkenes,such as ethene, are **unsaturated hydrocarbons** containing a double covalent bond between two carbon atoms.They are produced by cracking long chain alkanes.

The simplest alkene is ethene.

Alkenes can be distinguished from alkanes using a solution of bromine.

Alkanes do not decolourise bromine. Alkenes turn red bromine colourless.

The product of the reaction of bromine and ethene is 1,2-dibromoethane.

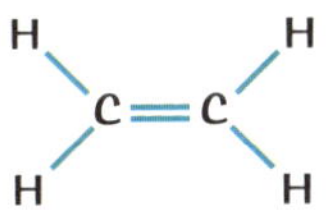

Ethene

Polymerisation

Alkene molecules are joined together to form long polymer chains. This process is called **polymerisation**. One example is poly(ethene).

The polymer is made by joining large numbers of ethene molecules together by a series of addition reactions.

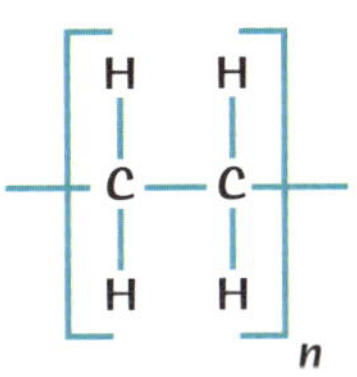

Carbohydrates

Carbohydrates are compounds of carbon,hydrogen and oxygen with a formula $C_x(H_2O)_y$. One example of a carbohydrate is sucrose (sugar) $C_{12}H_{22}O_{11}$.

By a process of **fermentation** enzymes in yeast convert sugar solution into ethanol, C_2H_5OH and carbon dioxide.

EXAM PRACTICE

1 Chloroethane and chloroethene are two organic carbon compounds.

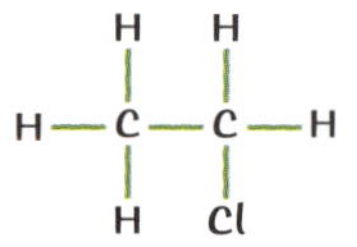

Chloroethane

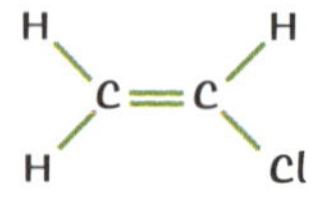

Chloroethene

a Describe how they could be distinguished by a chemical test. **3 marks**

b Chloroethene can be prepared by the reaction of ethyne with a gas.
The equation is:

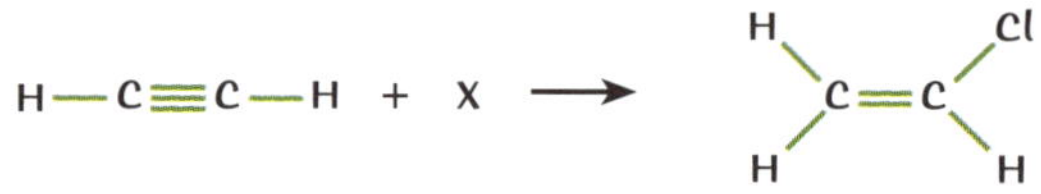

i) What is X? **1 mark**

ii) Put a ring around the best word from this list to describe the reaction taking place.

addition   combustion   oxidation   substitution **1 mark**

c Chloroethene when treated with a catalyst produces a white waxy solid.

i) Write down the name of this process. **1 mark**

ii) Finish the equation:

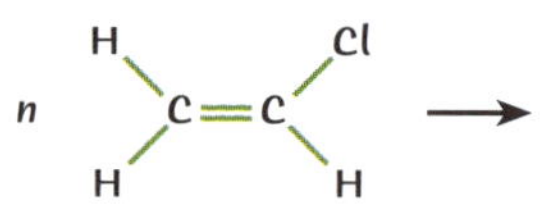

2 marks

d This white waxy solid can be made into plates and beakers to take on picnics.
Why is this material better than cardboard for these products? **2 marks**

2 Pentane is a member of the alkane family containing five carbon atoms.

a Write down the molecular formula of pentane. **1 mark**

b Draw the three structures of alkanes containing five carbon atoms. **3 marks**

3 Much household rubbish is tipped into landfill tips. Methane, CH_4, is often found underground in these tips.

a Why can a build-up of this gas be dangerous? **1 mark**

b The products of combustion of methane depend upon conditions.
Explain this statement.
Include balanced symbol equations in your answer. **4 marks**

4 How was petroleum formed underground millions of years ago?
How is it trapped underground? **6 marks**

Revision Unit 14

Metals

The Check Up

Potassium – most reactive
Sodium
Calcium
Magnesium
Aluminium
carbon
Zinc
Iron
Lead
hydrogen
Copper
Silver – least reactive

1 What is the name of the list of common metals in order of decreasing reactivity?

____

2 Write down the name of a common ore of aluminium. ____________

3 How is aluminium extracted from pure alumina? ____________

4 Why is the alumina dissolved in molten cryolite rather than just melted?

____

5 Finish the equations for the reactions in the extraction of aluminium.

Al^{3+} + ____ ⟶ ____

____ O^{2-} ⟶ ____ + $4e^-$

6 Write down the common name of an ore of iron. ____________

7 What two substances are added to the blast furnace with iron ore?

____________ and ____________

8 What is the active reducing agent in the blast furnace? ____________

9 What is tapped from the furnace in addition to molten iron? ____________

10 What is most of the iron from the blast furnace turned into? ____________

11 Why is one method used to extract aluminium and a different method used to extract iron?

____

12 What gas is formed when a metal reacts with dilute acid? ____________

13 Write down the name of a metal which reacts with steam but not with cold water. ____________

14 Write down the name of a metal which does not react with steam or dilute acid. ____________

15 What is formed when zinc is added to copper(II) sulphate solution?

____________ and ____________

16 What type of reaction is taking place in question 15? ____________

17 What name is given to a mixture of metals such as brass? ____________

18 Write down the names of four possible starting materials for producing magnesium sulphate using sulphuric acid.

____

19 What method is used to make insoluble salts? ____________

20 Write down the ionic equation for a neutralisation reaction. ____________

Mark yourself *(see answers on page 114)*

- More than 12? Do the exam practice – or go onto another unit.
- Less than 12? Do the crash course on the next page.

/20

THE CRASH COURSE

Metals and non-metals

Elements can be divided into metals and non-metals.

Metals burn in oxygen to form oxides with pH values of 7 or above (neutral or alkaline).

Reactivity series

Metals can be arranged in order of reactivity in the **reactivity series** (see page 63).

This table gives the reactions of common metals with air, water and dilute acids.

Metal	Reaction with air	Reaction with water	Reaction with dilute hydrochloric acid
potassium	burn in air or oxygen to form an oxide	reacts violently with cold water to produce hydrogen; hydrogen burns with a lilac flame	violent reaction to produce hydrogen (dangerous)
sodium		reacts quickly with cold water to produce hydrogen; hydrogen does not ignite	
calcium		reacts slowly with cold water to produce hydrogen	
magnesium		reacts very slowly with cold water; violent reaction with steam	react with acid to produce a metal chloride and hydrogen; react more slowly down list
zinc		fairly fast with steam	
iron		reacts only reversibly with steam	
lead	converted to the oxide by heating in air or oxygen but do not burn	no reaction with water or steam	exceedingly slow reaction to produce hydrogen
copper			hydrogen not produced; no reaction with dilute hydrochloric acid
silver	not affected by oxygen or air		

A metal will replace a less reactive metal in a compound. This is a **displacement reaction**, e.g. $Fe + CuSO_4 \longrightarrow Cu + FeSO_4$

Extraction of metals

The method used to extract a metal from its **ores** depends upon the position of the metal in the reactivity series.

Metals high in the reactivity series form stable compounds and these can only be split up by electrolysis.

Metals in the middle of the reactivity series are usually extracted by reduction using carbon.

Metals low in the reactivity series are obtained by heating the ore or may be found uncombined in the Earth.

THE CRASH COURSE

Extraction of aluminium

This diagram summarises the extraction of aluminium from alumina by **electrolysis**.

Aluminium oxide melts at a very high temperature. Aluminium oxide dissolved in molten cryolite gives a conducting solution at about 900 °C.

Positively charged aluminium ions are discharged at the negative cathode by gaining electrons.

Negatively charged oxide ions are discharged at the positive anode by losing electrons.

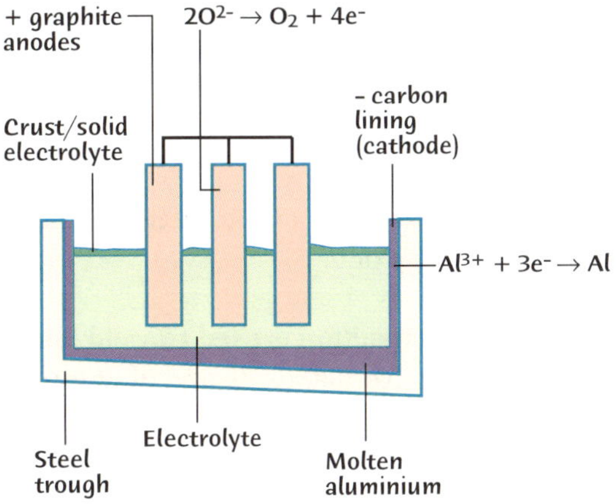

Extraction of aluminium by electrolysis

Extraction of iron

This diagram summarises the extraction of iron by reduction.

Iron ore (mainly haematite), coke and limestone are fed into the top of the furnace.

Oxygen from the hot air blast **oxidises** the coke to form carbon dioxide - equation (a).

The carbon dioxide is **reduced** to carbon monoxide by reacting with more coke - equation (b).

The carbon monoxide reduces the iron oxide in the ore to iron - equation (c).

Limestone is decomposed into calcium oxide and carbon monoxide - equation (d).

Calcium oxide reacts with impurities to form slag - equation (e).

The high temperature melts the iron and slag. They are tapped off at the bottom of the furnace.

(a) $C + O_2 \rightarrow CO_2$

(b) $CO_2 + C \rightarrow 2CO$

(c) $3CO + Fe_2O_3 \rightarrow 2Fe + 3CO_2$

(d) $CaCO_3 \rightarrow CaO + CO_2$

(e) $CaO + SiO_2 \rightarrow CaSiO_3$

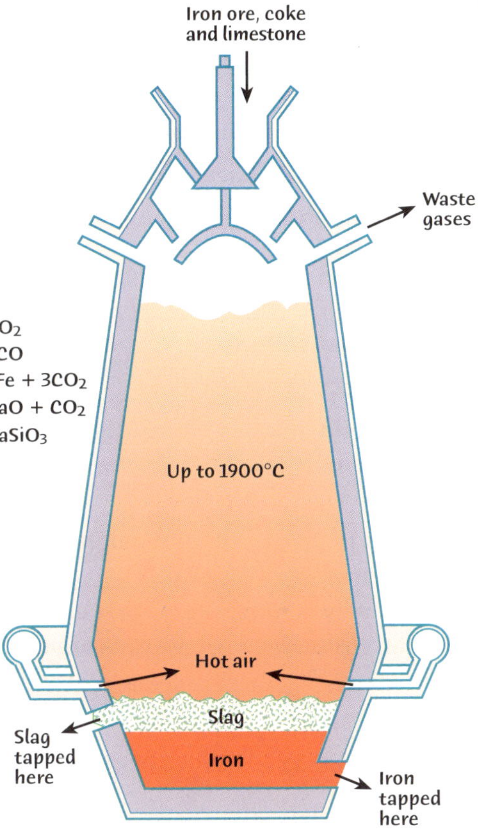

Extraction of iron in a blast furnace

Salt formation

A **salt** is produced when hydrogen in an acid is replaced by a metal.

Soluble salts are prepared by the reaction of metal, metal oxide, metal hydroxide or metal carbonate with the appropriate acid.

Insoluble salts are prepared by **precipitation**.

Mixing an acid and an alkali in appropriate amounts produces a neutral solution. This process is called **neutralisation**. The ionic equation for neutralisation is $H^+ + OH^- \rightarrow H_2O$

EXAM PRACTICE

1 Copper(II) sulphate crystals can be prepared by the reaction of dilute sulphuric acid, H_2SO_4, with solid black copper(II) oxide.

a Write a balanced symbol equation for the reaction producing copper(II) sulphate crystals. 2 marks

b Write an account of the method used to prepare copper(II) sulphate crystals from copper(II) oxide. 6 marks

2 The thermit reaction is used to weld lengths of railway track together. A mixture of iron(III) oxide and aluminium powder is placed between the two lengths of track and set alight. The heat generated welds the track together.

a What type of reaction is taking place when iron(III) oxide and aluminium react? 1 mark

b Write a balanced symbol equation for the reaction. 2 marks

c Which metal in the list would be best to use if aluminium was not available? 1 mark

copper lead magnesium sodium

3 a Choose words from this list to complete the sentences.

calcium oxide carbon monoxide coke ore reduction slag steel

Iron is extracted from iron ______ by a process of __________ .
The blast furnace is loaded with iron ore, _______ and limestone. Hot air is blown into the furnace.
The reducing agent is _________ .
Limestone splits up into _____________ which reacts with impurities in the furnace to form ______ . This is tapped off. Most of the iron produced in the furnace is turned into _______ . 6 marks

b Explain how limestone ($CaCO_3$) is used to remove impurities, e.g. silicon(IV) oxide (SiO_2), from iron ore in the blast furnace. Include balanced chemical equations in your answer. 4 marks

c It is important that as much carbon dioxide as possible is produced in the blast furnace.

i) Why is it important that carbon dioxide is produced? 1 mark
ii) Write down two ways in which carbon dioxide is produced in the furnace. 2 marks

Revision Unit 15

Rates of reaction and equilibrium

The Check Up

1 In a series of reactions the time taken gets longer from one reaction to the next. What happens to the rate?

2 What is a catalyst?

3 Why are only small amount of catalysts usually required?

4 What name is given to a biological catalyst?

5 Why is coal dust explosive in a coal mine but the lumps of coal are not?

6 Which would react faster – magnesium ribbon and hydrochloric acid (1 mol/dm^3) or magnesium ribbon and hydrochloric acid (2 mol/dm^3)?

7 A mixture of hydrogen and chlorine explodes in sunlight. Why?

8 Food kept in a deep freezer does not go bad as quickly as it would at room temperature. Why?

9 The rusting of a steel ship takes place faster in the tropics than it does in Great Britain. Why?

10 Why, in terms of particles, does raising the temperature speed up the rate of the reaction?

11 What name is given to the situation when the concentrations of products and reactants remain unchanged in a reversible reaction but both forward and reverse reactions continue at the same rate?

These questions refer to the industrial process producing ammonia from nitrogen and hydrogen.

12 What is the name of this process?

13 Write a balanced symbol equation for the process.

14 How is the nitrogen needed for the process obtained?

15 How is the hydrogen needed for the process obtained?

16 What is the catalyst used in the process?

17 What happens to the unreacted nitrogen and hydrogen?

18 How is the ammonia removed from the reaction mixture?

19 What conditions of temperature and pressure give the best yield of ammonia?

20 What is the name and formula of the fertiliser produced when ammonia and sulphuric acid react?

Mark yourself *(see answers on page 115)*

- More than 12? Do the exam practice – or go onto another unit.
- Less than 12? Do the crash course on the next page.

/ 20

THE CRASH COURSE

Rate of reaction and time

Chemical reactions take place at very different speeds.
A reaction which takes a short period of time is a fast reaction and one that takes a long time is a slow reaction.

$$\text{Rate} = \frac{1}{\text{time}}$$

Factors which affect the rate of reactions

Rate is increased by:

- increasing the concentration of one or more reactants
- increasing the temperature
- increasing the surface area of a solid
- adding a catalyst
- increasing the pressure (for reactions involving gases).

When investigating the effect of changing one of these factors it is necessary to keep all others the same.

Catalysts

A **catalyst** is a substance which alters the rate of a chemical reaction without being used up. A common example is manganese(IV) oxide which catalyses the decomposition of hydrogen peroxide into water and oxygen.

Enzymes are biological catalysts.

Changes in rate of reaction can be explained in terms of **particles**.

Increasing temperature or increasing concentration (or pressure in the case of gases) increases the number of collisions. More frequent and energetic collisions mean more effective collisions and therefore a faster reaction.

Reversible reactions and equilibrium

Some reactions do not convert all of the reactants into the products. The products split up to reform the reactants. This is a **reversible** reaction.

A reversible reaction is recognised by a $\rightleftharpoons$ sign.

If a reversible reaction takes place in a closed system where substances cannot escape an **equilibrium** can be set up.

In an equilibrium the forward and reverse reactions are taking place at the same rates so no reaction appears to be occurring.

An equilibrium is a delicate balance and slight changes to the conditions can alter the rate of the forward or reverse reaction and alter the **position of the equilibrium**.

THE CRASH COURSE

The Haber process

The Haber process to manufacture ammonia from nitrogen and hydrogen is the common example you need to know.

Nitrogen is produced from the fractional distillation of liquid air and hydrogen by the reaction of methane (natural gas) or naphtha with steam.

The mixture of nitrogen and hydrogen is passed over a heated iron catalyst.

Some nitrogen and hydrogen combine to form ammonia

$$N_2(g) + 3H_2(g) \rightleftharpoons 2NH_3(g)$$

Ammonia is removed by liquefying and unreacted nitrogen and hydrogen are recycled.

Ammonia produced is turned into fertilisers, e.g. ammonium sulphate, $(NH_4)_2SO_4$.

EXAM PRACTICE

1 Sue carried out a series of reactions with marble chips and excess hydrochloric acid.

$$CaCO_3(s) + 2HCl(aq) \longrightarrow CaCl_2(aq) + H_2O(l) + CO_2(g)$$

She collected the total volume of gas produced each half minute.

The first experiment produced the graph line labelled **A**.

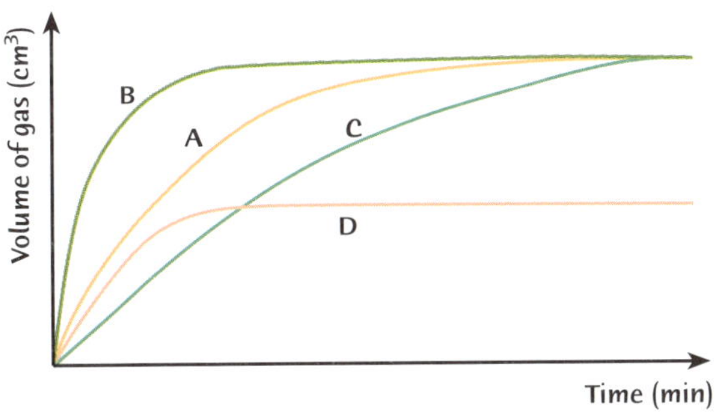

a She repeated the experiment but used half the mass of marble chips. Other conditions were the same.

Which graph line was obtained from this experiment?

Explain your choice. **3 marks**

b In the final experiment she used the same mass of marble chips and the same conditions as the first experiment. She crushed the marble chips into a coarse powder.

Which graph line was obtained from this experiment? Explain your choice. **3 marks**

c Describe how she could measure the rate in this reaction without measuring gas volumes. **3 marks**

Continued ▶

Exam Practice

2 Hydrogen peroxide is decomposed into water and oxygen.

$2H_2O_2(aq) \longrightarrow 2H_2O(l) + O_2(g)$

Ali carries out an experiment to decompose a 25 cm³ sample of hydrogen peroxide solution with 1 spatula measure of manganese(IV) oxide. The experiment was carried out at room temperature.
Here are her results.

Time (min)	0	1	2	3	4	5
Volume of gas collected (cm^3)	0	25	40	48	50	50

a Draw a labelled diagram of the apparatus she could use for this experiment. **3 marks**

b Use the grid to draw a graph of her results. **4 marks**

c She repeated the experiment but mixed the hydrogen peroxide with an equal volume of water before adding the manganese(IV) oxide.

i) On the same grid sketch the graph she would expect to get in this experiment. **2 marks**

ii) Explain, in terms of particles, why she expected this shape of graph. **2 marks**

d The concentration of hydrogen peroxide solution is sometimes measured as 'volume strength'.

A 10-volume solution produces 10 cm^3 of oxygen for each 1 cm^3 of solution used.

What is the volume strength of the hydrogen peroxide Ali used? **1 mark**

e Other substances were tested as possible catalysts.

Substances that worked: lead(IV) oxide, copper(II) oxide, chromium(III) oxide.

Substances that did not work: magnesium oxide, calcium oxide, zinc oxide.

Suggest why some substances act as catalysts and some do not. **2 marks**

f Catalase also acts as a catalyst for this reaction at temperatures up to about 45°C.

i) What type of catalyst is catalase? **1 mark**

ii) Why does catalase not act as a catalyst at higher temperatures? **1 mark**

Revision Unit 16

Rocks of the Earth and Earth cycles

The Check Up

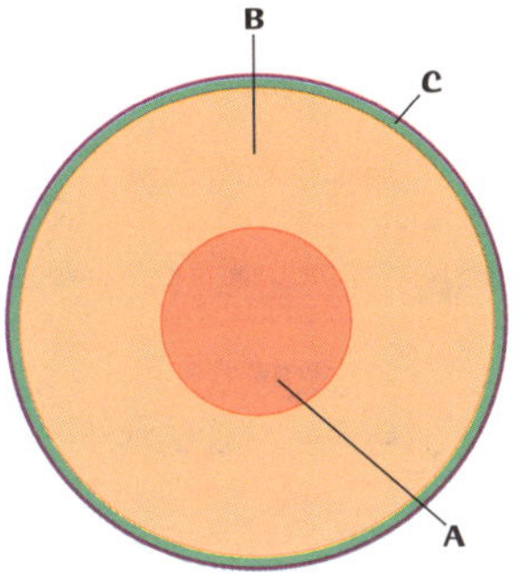

1 Label the three parts of the Earth **A**, **B** and **C**.

A ____________________ **B** ____________________ **C** ____________________

2 What type of rock is formed when magma crystallises and forms solid rock?

____

Use this list of common rocks to answer Questions 3 and 4.

basalt conglomerate granite limestone marble

3 Write down the name of a metamorphic rock. ____________________

4 Write down the name of a sedimentary rock. ____________________

5 Basalt is an extrusive rock and granite is an intrusive rock. What is the meaning of the terms extrusive and intrusive? ____________________

6 What does crystal size show about the rate of cooling of rocks? ____________________

____

7 What conditions turn sedimentary rocks into metamorphic rocks? ____________________

____

8 Write down the names of four processes involved in breaking down rocks and producing sedimentary rocks.

____

9 In which type of rocks are fossils never found? ____________________

10 Which scientist was responsible for the modern theory of plate tectonics? ____________________

11 Where does the energy come from to drive the rock cycle? ____________________

12 Why do many earthquakes take place on plate boundaries? ____________________

13 Why are Europe and the United States of America very slowly getting further apart? ____________________

____

14 How is a range of mountains like the Himalayas formed? ____________________

____

15 Write down the names of three processes which take oxygen out of the air.

____

16 Write down the name of a process which replaces carbon dioxide in the air with oxygen. ____________________

17 Millions of years ago the composition of the Earth's atmosphere was very different from what it is now. What change in composition occurred as the green plants started to grow widely? ____________________

____

18 In the past 100 years the composition of the atmosphere has changed with more carbon dioxide in the atmosphere. What has caused this increase in carbon dioxide? ____________________

____

At a destructive plate boundary, one plate is forced under another.

19 Which plate is forced underneath? ____________________

20 What happens to the plate forced underneath? ____________________

Mark yourself *(see answers on page 116)*

- More than 12? Do the exam practice – or go onto another unit.
- Less than 12? Do the crash course below.

/20

THE CRASH COURSE

The structure of the Earth

The Earth is made up of several parts.

At the centre of the Earth is the **core**. This can be divided into the inner core and the outer core.

Around the core is the **mantle**.

Exposed to the atmosphere is a thin layer of the Earth's **crust**.

Types of rock

Rocks can be classified as **igneous**, **sedimentary or metamorphic**.

Igneous rocks are formed when magma from inside the Earth crystallises.

Igneous rocks are crystalline. If the cooling is slow large crystals are formed and if it is rapid small crystals are formed.

Igneous rocks crystallised inside the Earth are called **intrusive rocks**, e.g. granite.

Igneous rocks crystallised on the surface of the Earth are called **extrusive rocks**, e.g. basalt.

Rocks are worn away by processes of weathering and erosion.

These processes break up existing rocks into tiny fragments which can be **transported**, **deposited**, **compacted** and **cemented** together to form **sedimentary** rocks, e.g. limestone and sandstone.

Sedimentary rocks can be converted into **metamorphic** rocks by the action of high temperatures and/or high pressures. Marble is an example of a metamorphic rock.

Fossils are usually found in sedimentary rocks but sometimes in metamorphic rocks.

The rock cycle

The rock cycle (shown opposite) summarises the processes which produce and destroy rocks.

The rock cycle is driven by solar energy and the energy from nuclear reactions within the Earth.

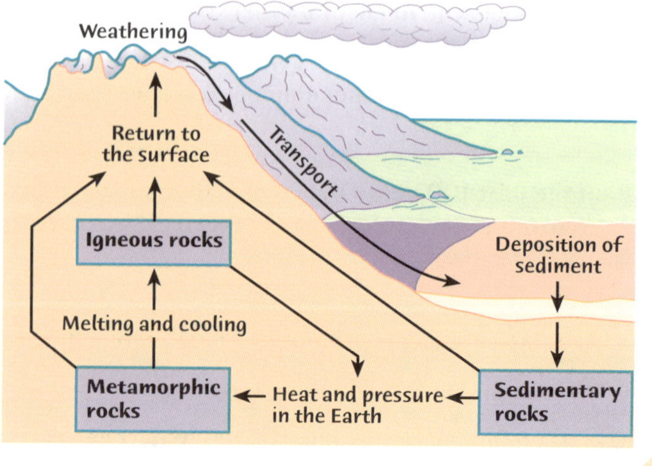

The Crash Course

Plate tectonics

Alfred Wegener proposed that the Earth's crust is made up a number of large plates.

The diagram below shows the plates of the Earth.

These plates were moving slowly.

Where two plates are moving together one plate may be pushed up to form mountains and one plate is pushed underneath returning rocks to the magma to be re-cycled.

At a constructive plate boundary new rocks are formed as molten rock from the magma comes to the surface.

Earthquakes occur when plates rub against each other.

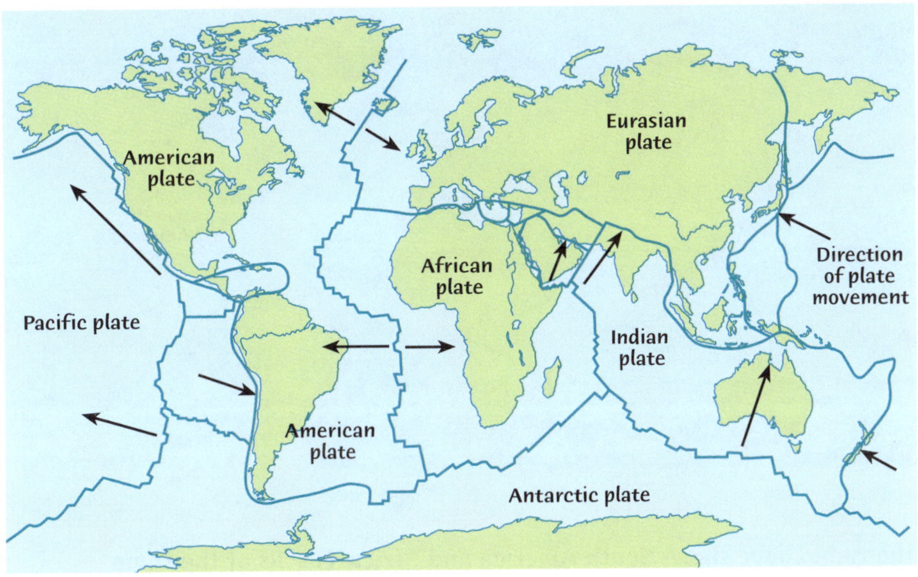

Earth's atmosphere

The present Earth's atmosphere consists of about 79% nitrogen and 20% oxygen with smaller amounts of carbon dioxide, water vapour and noble gases, e.g. argon, neon and krypton.

Millions of years ago the Earth's atmosphere had large quantities of carbon dioxide and small amounts of oxygen. As green plants became established **photosynthesis** reduced concentration of carbon dioxide and increased the concentration of oxygen.

In the past one hundred years, increased burning of fossil fuels, such as coal and oil, has increased carbon dioxide levels and decreased oxygen levels.

Exam Practice

1 This diagram shows some of the steps in the rock cycle. **7 marks**

Choose words from this list to label each of the stages. You can use words once, more than once or not at all.

compacting crystallising erosion

high temperature and high pressure melting

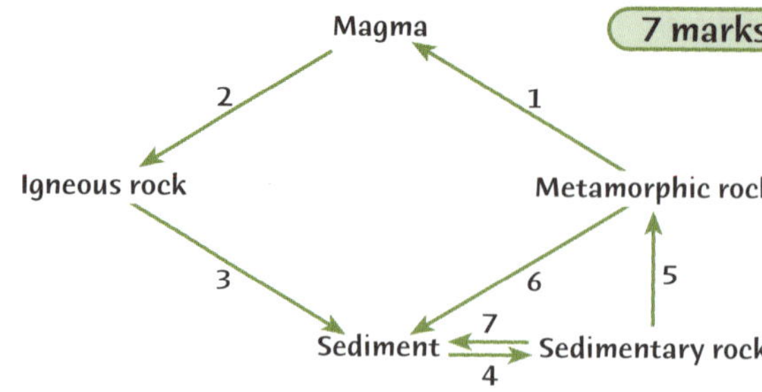

2 This diagram on the left below shows places where earthquakes have been recorded.

What is the significance of this pattern of earthquakes? **2 marks**

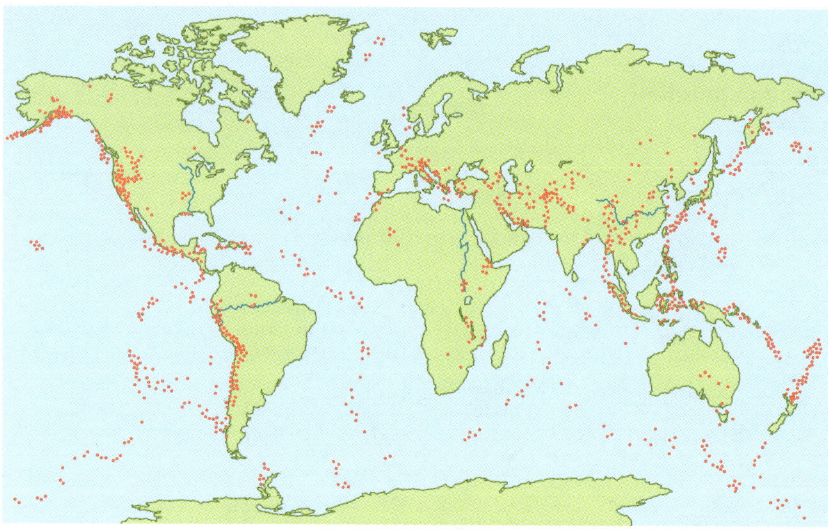

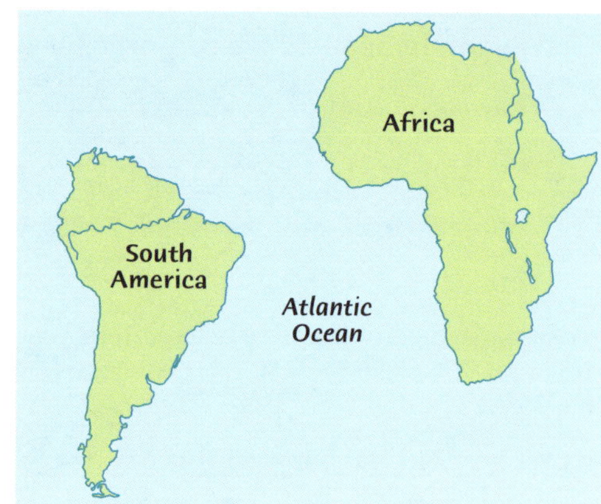

3 The diagram on the right above shows South America and Africa. Fossils of the same species of a reptile are found on both continents. How does the theory of plate tectonics explain this? **2 marks**

4 At a plate boundary two plates are colliding. The continental plate is about 35 km thick and has an average density of 2.7 g/cm^3. The oceanic plate is much thinner and has a density of 3.3 g/cm^3. The material under the crust has a density of 4.5 g/cm^3.

Describe what will happen when the continental and oceanic plates collide. A diagram may help your answer. **4 marks**

5 Millions of years ago iron(II) carbonate rocks were converted into iron(III) oxide. Explain how this altered the composition of the atmosphere. A balanced equation with state symbols should be included in your answer. **6 marks**

6 This diagram shows a section through the Earth's crust. Use the letters A–E to answer these questions.

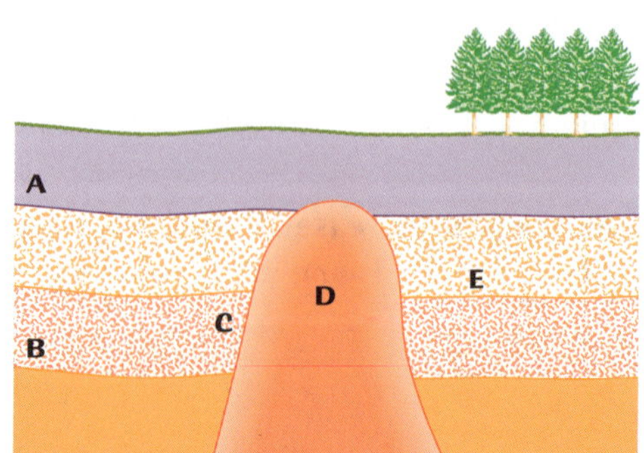

a Which rock is the oldest sedimentary rock? **1 mark**

b Where would intrusive igneous rock be likely to form? **1 mark**

c Where would metamorphic rock be likely to form? **1 mark**

d Where would there be no chance of finding fossils? **1 mark**

Revision Unit 11

Current and circuits

The Check Up

1 What is the difference between a series circuit and a parallel circuit?

____

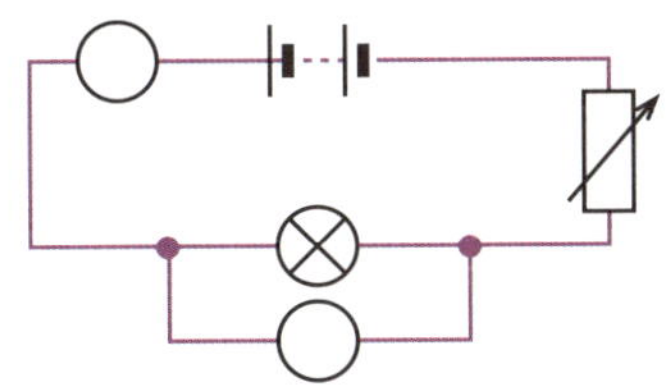

2 Complete the symbols for the ammeter and voltmeter on this circuit diagram.

3 What does the symbol  represent and what job does it do?

4 Complete this sentence. The current in the circuit shown transfers

__________ from the __________ to the __________.

5 Why are household lamps normally connected in parallel? __________

6 What is the unit of resistance? Give the name and the symbol. __________

7 Which circuit component allows current to pass in one direction only? __________

8 Which circuit component has a resistance that goes down as the temperature goes up? __________

9 Which circuit component has a resistance that depends on the light intensity? __________

10 Complete the labels for this diagram of a plug.

A __________ B __________ C __________ D __________

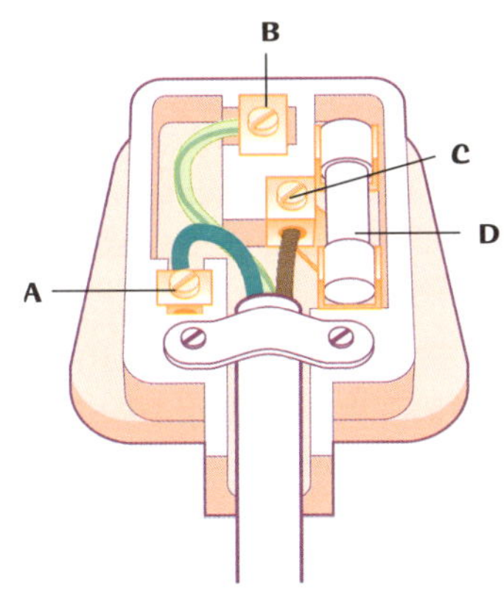

Wiring in a 3-pin plug

11 What is the purpose of the fuse? __________

12 Which wire supplies the appliance with energy? __________

13 Which wire does not have any current passing in it when the appliance is working normally? __________

14 Which two parts of the plug protect the user against electrocution?

____

15 What is the difference between alternating current (a.c.) and direct current (d.c.)?

____

16 A current of 2.5 A passes in a 6.8 Ω resistor. Work out the voltage across the resistor.

____

17 The current in a filament lamp is 0.50 A when the voltage across it is 6.0 V. Work out the resistance of the filament. __________

18 What happens to the resistance of a lamp filament when the current in it is increased? __________

19 Calculate the power input to a kettle if the current in the element is 8.5 A when the voltage across it is 240 V.

____

20 Use the formula *energy transfer in kWh* = *power in kW* × *time in h* to calculate the cost of using a 2 kW heater for two hours each day for a week. The cost of each kWh of energy is 7 p.

____

Mark yourself *(see answers on page 116)*

- More than 12? Do the exam practice – or go onto another unit.
- Less than 12? Do the crash course on the next page.

/ 20

The Crash Course

Circuits

A **series** circuit has only one current path. A **parallel** circuit has more than one current path.

The current in a series circuit has the same value everywhere. In a parallel circuit, the total current passing into a junction is equal to the current that passes out of the junction.

A battery, power supply or the mains provides the energy input to a circuit. This energy is transferred by the current to the components.

The size of the **current** passing in a circuit is affected both by the **voltage** and the **resistance** of the circuit.

Current is measured by connecting an **ammeter** in series in the circuit; voltage is measured by connecting a **voltmeter** in parallel with a battery or a component.

Components

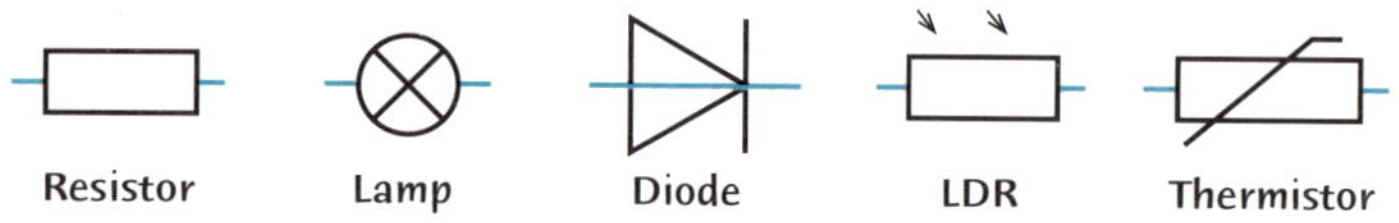

The current passing in a metallic conductor is directly proportional to the voltage across it provided that the temperature remains the same. The resistance has a constant value.

If the temperature of the metallic conductor increases, so does its resistance. This happens in a lamp filament.

A **diode** allows current to pass in one direction only.

The resistance of a **light-dependent resistor (LDR)** falls as the light level increases. That of a **thermistor** falls as the temperature increases.

Mains electricity

Mains electricity is **alternating current** (a.c.), i.e. the current changes direction. The electric current from a battery is **direct current** (d.c.), i.e. it always passes in the same direction.

Three conductors are used to connect an appliance to the mains supply. Each can be identified by the colour of its insulation (see diagram).

The **live** wire provides the energy from the mains supply.

The **neutral** wire is there to make a complete circuit; the same current passes in the neutral wire as in the live wire.

The **fuse** and **earth** wire are for safety. The fuse on its own protects against fire in the cable by breaking the circuit if the current becomes too great.

The earth wire is connected to any exposed metal parts of the appliance. If they become live a large current passes to earth, causing the fuse to break the circuit.

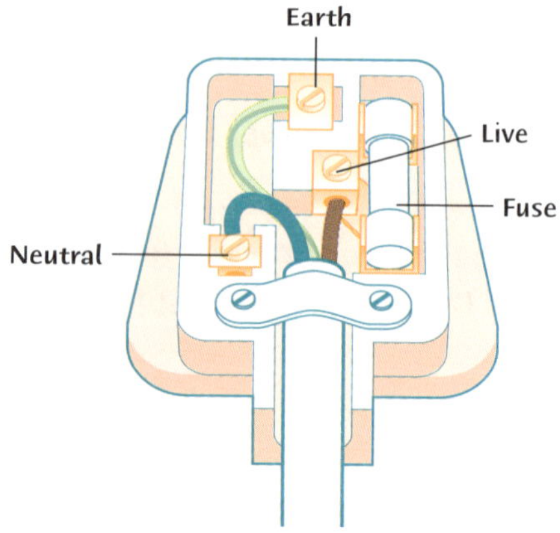

Wiring in a 3-pin plug

THE CRASH COURSE

Circuit calculations

These formulae show the relationships between voltage, current, power and energy transfer:

voltage = current × resistance $V = I \times R$

power = current × voltage $P = I \times V$

energy transfer = power x time $E = P \times t$*

*this formula will be provided on the examination paper

EXAM PRACTICE

1 Write down the readings on ammeters **A1**, **A2** and **A3** and voltmeters **V1** and **V2**. 5 marks

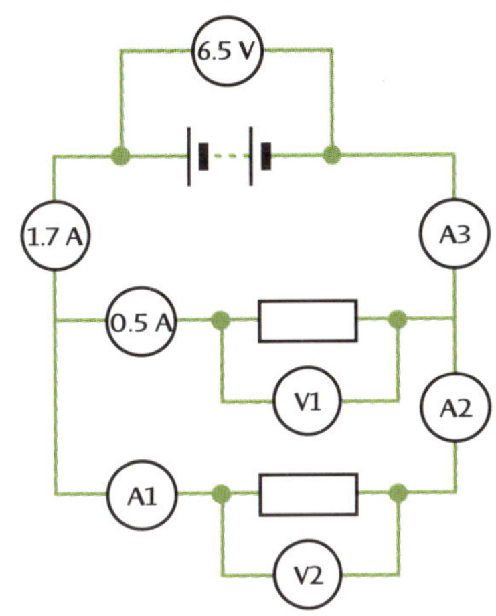

2 An electric toaster is connected to the 240 V mains supply.
When switched on and operating normally, the current in the element is 3.8 A.

a Calculate the power of the element. 3 marks

b Which of the following fuses should be fitted to the plug?

1 A   3 A   5 A   10 A   13 A

Explain why this fuse is the most suitable. 2 marks

c Calculate the resistance of the element when it is operating normally. 3 marks

d Explain why the current is likely to be greater than 3.8 A when the toaster is first switched on. 2 marks

e i) Which part of the toaster should the earth wire be connected to? 1 mark

ii) If the heating element breaks, part of it could touch the metal case. Why could this be a danger to the user? 1 mark

iii) Explain how the fuse and the earth wire together protect the user against this danger. 2 marks

f i) A television set has a plastic case.
There are only two conductors in the connection to the mains supply.
Which conductor is missing?
Explain why this conductor is not necessary. 3 marks

ii) The power rating of the television is 160 W.
Calculate the energy transfer from the mains when the television is switched on for 8 hours.
Give your answer in kWh.
Use the formula: *energy transfer = power × time* 2 marks

iii) Calculate the cost of using the television set for 8 hours if the cost of each kWh is 7 p. 1 mark

Revision Unit 18

Charge, current and magnetism

The Check Up

1 State the rule for attraction and repulsion between charged objects. ____________________

2 Explain how polythene becomes negatively charged when it is rubbed with a duster.

____

3 Why is it more difficult to charge copper by rubbing with a duster than it is to charge polythene?

____

4 Static charge can build up when aircraft are being refuelled. Why is this dangerous?

____

5 What is the job of an electrostatic precipitator in a power station? ____________________

6 Complete the sentence:

The current in a metallic conductor is due to a movement of __________ from __________ to __________ .

7 How is the current in a conducting gas different to that in a metallic conductor?

____

8 A current of 4.5 A passes in a battery. How much charge flows through the battery in 30 s? ____________________

9 State the rule for attraction and repulsion between magnetic poles. ____________________

10 What do the arrows on a magnetic field diagram represent? ____________________

11 The diagram opposite shows the force on a wire that is carrying a current at right angles to a magnetic field.

State **two** ways of reversing the direction of the force. ____________________

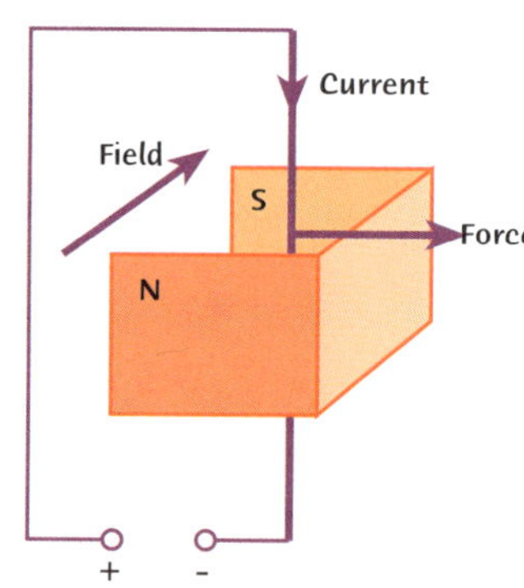

12 Use the information in question 11 to draw arrows that show the forces acting on the left-hand side and right-hand side of the coil in the diagram below.

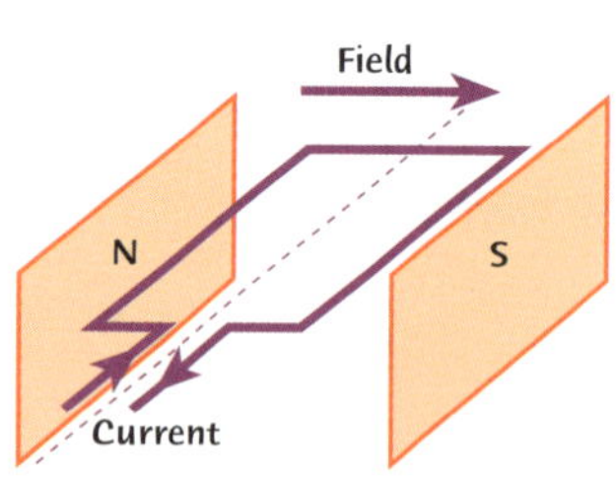

For questions 13–15
The diagram opposite shows a coil of wire connected to a sensitive voltmeter, and a magnet.

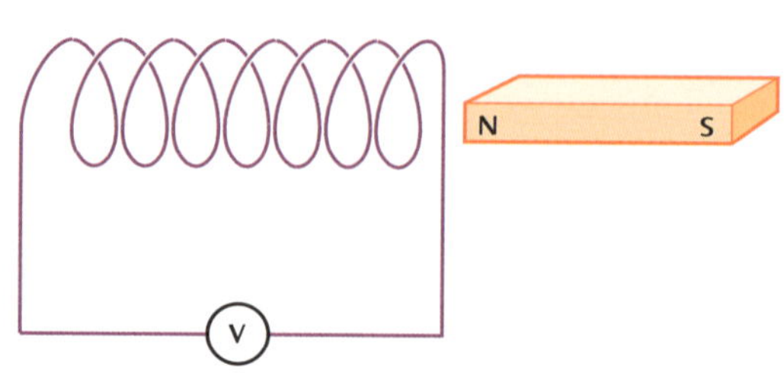

13 How can a voltage be induced in the coil of wire? ____________________

14 State **two** factors that affect the size of the induced voltage. ____________________

15 State **two** ways of reversing the direction of the induced voltage. ____________________

Continued ▶

The Check Up

16 What is the job of a step-up transformer? ______

17 How is the construction of a step-up transformer different to that of a step-down transformer?

______

18 At a power station, electricity is generated at 25 000 V.

The voltage is then increased to 400 000 V.

The primary coil has 1000 turns. How many turns does the secondary coil have? ______

19 Why is electricity transmitted at high voltage? ______

20 How is the voltage reduced for safe domestic and commercial use? ______

Mark yourself *(see answers on page 117)*

- More than 12? Do the exam practice – or go onto another unit.
- Less than 12? Do the crash course below.

/20

The Crash Course

Static charge

When two objects rub together, electrons are transferred from the surface of one to the surface of the other.

The object that **gains electrons** becomes **negatively charged**, and the object that **loses electrons** becomes **positively charged**.

Insulators retain this charge. Unless a **conductor** is isolated from the earth and other objects, the charge passes through it.

Objects with **similar charges repel each other**, and those with **opposite charges attract each other**.

Where there is a build-up of static charge, it creates a high voltage that can cause sparking.

Static charges are useful in attracting small particles in photocopying machines and in removing dust from power station exhaust gases.

Charge in motion

Moving charge is an electric current.

Charge flow = current × time

$Q = I \times t$

In a conducting metal, the current is due to a flow of free electrons from negative to positive.

In conducting gases and liquids, the current is due to a flow of both negatively and positively charged ions in opposite directions.

The Crash Course

Magnetic forces

Permanent magnets have **poles**, the places where the magnetism is strongest.

Two **north-seeking** or two **south-seeking** poles repel each other. Opposite poles attract each other.

Magnetic fields are regions around magnets and electric currents where there are magnetic forces. The direction of the magnetic field is the direction of the force on a north-seeking pole.

There is a force on an electric current passing at right angles to a magnetic field. The direction of this force is at right angles to both the current and the magnetic field (see the diagram on p. 78).

A **simple motor** (as shown below) uses the magnetic force on an electric current to produce rotation.

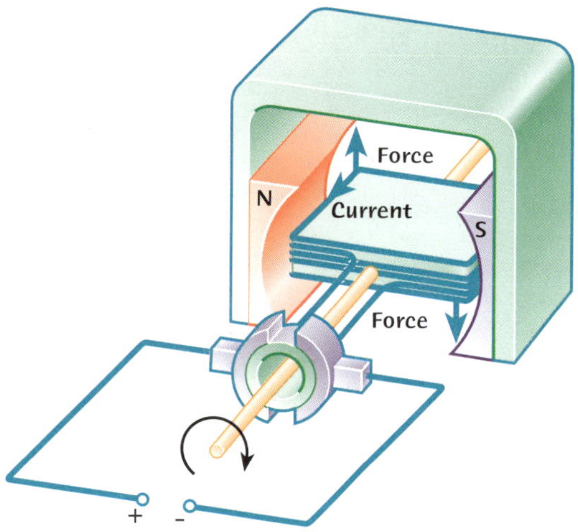

A simple motor

Electromagnetic induction

A voltage is **induced** across a conductor when it passes across a magnetic field or when the magnetic field through it changes.

The size of the induced voltage depends on the speed of the change and the speed of the conductor.

The direction of the induced voltage is reversed by reversing the change of magnetic field or reversing the movement of the conductor.

In a **generator**, a voltage is induced across a coil of wire when a magnet spins around inside it.

In a **transformer**, the changing magnetic field due to an alternating current in one coil of wire induces a voltage in an adjacent coil.

The relationship between the voltages and numbers of turns of wire on the transformer coils is:

$$\frac{\textit{primary voltage}}{\textit{secondary voltage}} = \frac{\textit{number of primary turns}}{\textit{number of secondary turns}}$$

Electricity is transmitted at high voltage and low current to reduce energy losses. Transformers are used to change the size of the voltage.

EXAM PRACTICE

1 a A person holds a polythene bag in one hand and rubs the surface with a cloth held in the other hand. The bag becomes negatively charged.
Explain how both the bag and the cloth become charged. (2 marks)

b The person now holds a copper strip and rubs it with the cloth.
i) Explain why the copper strip does not become charged. (2 marks)
ii) Explain whether the cloth becomes charged. (1 mark)
iii) What would the person have to do in order to charge the copper by rubbing? (1 mark)

2 a A simple circuit consists of a battery and a filament lamp.
In 60 s, 9.0 C of charge passes through the filament.
i) Calculate the current in the filament. (3 marks)
ii) What particles carry the charge in the circuit and what is their direction of flow? (2 marks)

b Neon lamps are often used to show when an appliance is switched on. Neon gas gives out light when an electric current passes in it.
What particles are responsible for the charge flow through the neon and what is their direction of flow? (2 marks)

3 a In a power station generator, a rotating electromagnet is surrounded by copper conductors.
i) Explain how this generates electricity. (2 marks)
ii) What **two** changes occur to the alternating voltage generated if the speed of the electromagnet changes? (2 marks)

b Before it passes into the grid, the electricity first goes through a step-up transformer.
i) Describe the construction of this transformer. (3 marks)
ii) What effect does the transformer have on the electric current? (1 mark)
iii) Explain how this helps to reduce energy losses during transmission. (2 marks)
iv) It is suggested that the electricity supply industry changes from using alternating current (a.c.) to using direct current (d.c.).
Discuss whether this would be feasible. (2 marks)

Revision Unit 19

Force and Pressure

The Check Up

1 The Earth's pull on the Moon is *less than/equal to/greater than* the Moon's pull on the Earth.

2 When a tractor pulls a trailer at a constant speed, the trailer *pulls/pushes* the tractor with a force that is *smaller/equal/greater* in size and in the *same/opposite* direction.

3 A person's weight is the force due to the ____________ *pulling/pushing* the ____________ .

This graph shows how the extension varies with the applied force for four different materials.

Use it to answer questions 4–7.

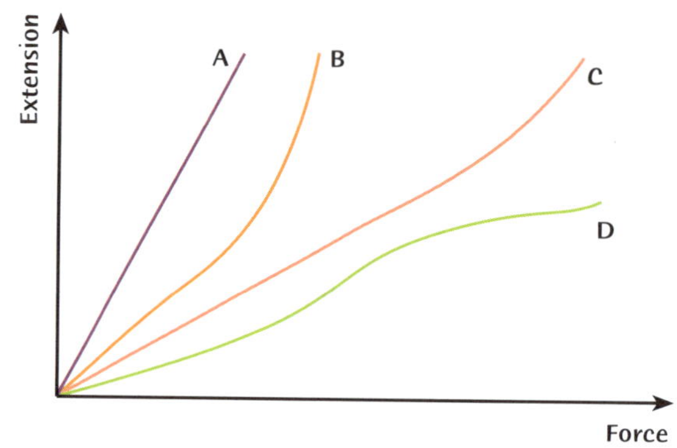

4 Which material is hardest to stretch? ____________

5 For which material is the extension always proportional to the force? ____________

6 Which material could be rubber? ____________

7 Which two materials could be copper **stretched** beyond its elastic limit? ____________

8 A spring is used in a forcemeter. Give **two** reasons why the elastic limit of the spring should not be exceeded.

____

9 Explain how a wire is able to cut through cheese. ____________

10 What pressure is exerted by a 600 N force acting over an area of 0.5 m^2? ____________

11 Atmospheric pressure is 1.01×10^5 Pa. What size force does the atmosphere exert on a window that measures 2.5 m × 1.5 m? ____________

12 Explain how an empty tin can becomes crushed when the air is taken away from the inside.

____

13 A force of 120 N is used to cause a pressure of 2400 Pa. What area does the force act over? ____________

This diagram shows a hydraulic system.

Use it to answer questions 14–16.

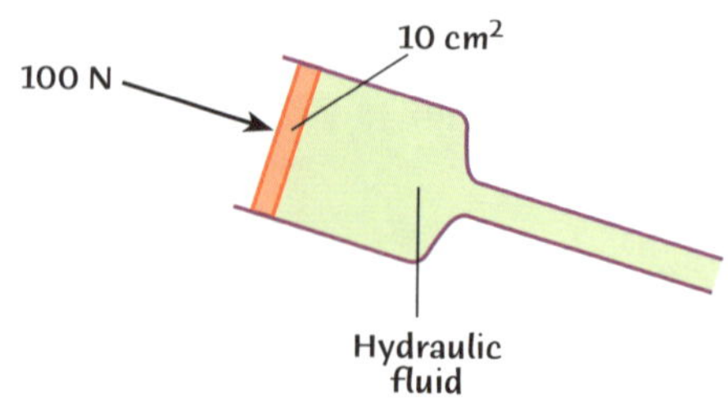

14 What pressure, in Pa, is exerted on the hydraulic fluid? ($1\ cm^2 = 1 \times 10^{-4} m^2$). ____________

15 In which direction or directions does the fluid transmit this pressure? ____________

16 Explain how a hydraulic system can be used to multiply forces. ____________

____

Continued ▶

The Check Up

17 Some carbon dioxide gas is inside a pressurised container. Explain how the gas exerts a pressure.

18 Explain how the pressure changes when some of the gas is released.

19 100 cm^3 of air is sealed in a syringe. The volume is reduced to 20 cm^3, while the temperature remains the same. What happens to the pressure? ______

20 Write down the formula that relates the initial pressure and volume of the gas to its final pressure and volume.

Mark yourself (see answers on page 118)

- More than 12? Do the exam practice – or go onto another unit.
- Less than 12? Do the crash course below.

/20

The Crash Course

Forces between objects

Forces can always be described as *object A pulls/pushes object B.*
If *object A pulls/pushes object B* then *object B pulls/pushes object A* with an **equal-sized force** acting in the **opposite direction**.

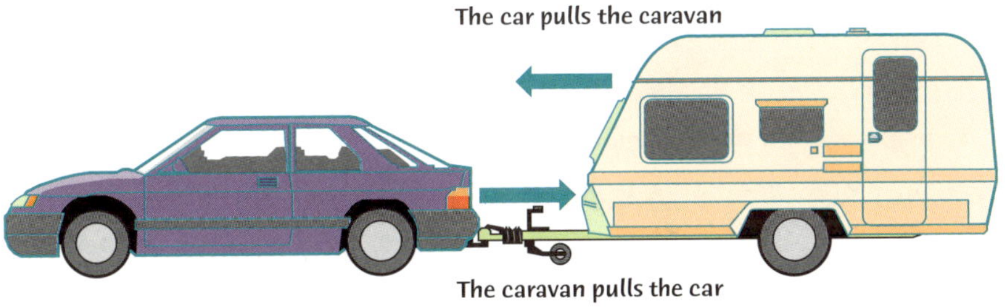

Force and extension

When a pulling force is applied to a spring or a wire, it stretches in a regular and predictable way.
Up to a certain limit, the extension is proportional to the force. This is known as **Hooke's Law**.
Beyond the limit, the extension increases out of proportion to the force and it may not return to its original size when the force is removed.
Rubber behaves differently; it becomes harder to stretch as the force is increased.

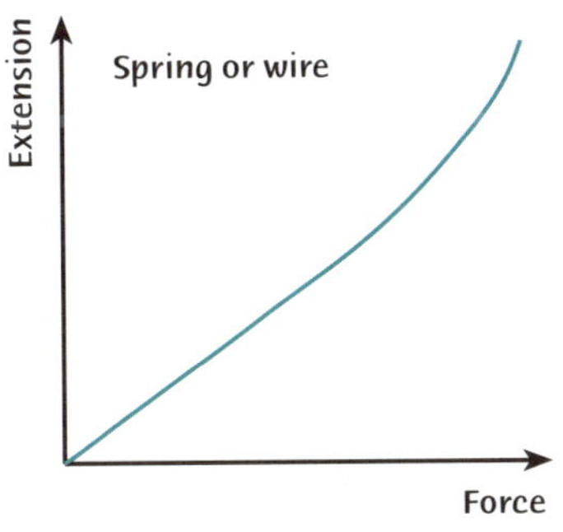

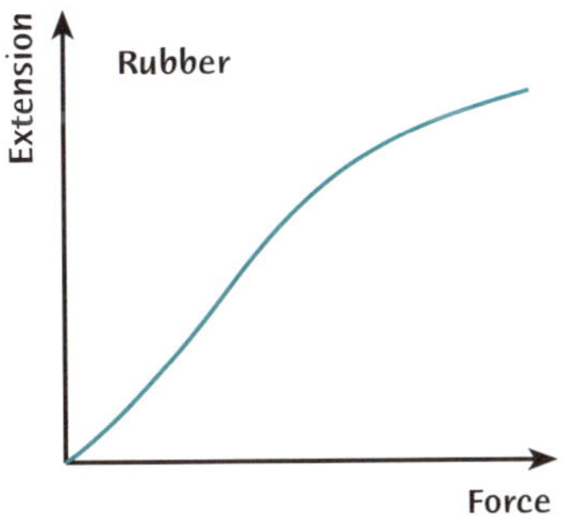

THE CRASH COURSE

Pressure in solids and liquids

Pressure is calculated as *force ÷ area*. It is measured in N/m^2 or Pa.

$$\text{Pressure} = \frac{\text{force}}{\text{area}}$$

The pressure acting on a solid is the effect that a force has in cutting or piercing.

Liquids transmit pressure equally in all directions.

Hydraulic machines use liquid pressure to magnify force or magnify movement.

Gas pressure

Gases exert pressure due to collisions between the particles of the gas and the walls of the container.

Reducing the volume of a gas increases the pressure owing to more frequent collisions.

The relationship between the pressure and volume of a fixed mass of gas at constant temperature is:

$$\text{pressure} \times \text{volume} = \text{constant} \quad \text{or} \quad P_1V_1 = P_2V_2{}^*$$

** this formula will be provided on examination papers*

EXAM PRACTICE

1 When a person stands on some weighing scales, a spring becomes compressed.

The diagram shows the two forces acting on the person.

a Write a description of each force shown on the diagram. **4 marks**

b Write a statement about the relative sizes of these forces.
Explain how you can tell. **2 marks**

Continued ▶

EXAM PRACTICE

2 The diagram shows part of a hydraulic machine.
A force of 150 N pushes on a piston that has an area of 7.5 cm^2 (7.5×10^{-4} m^2).

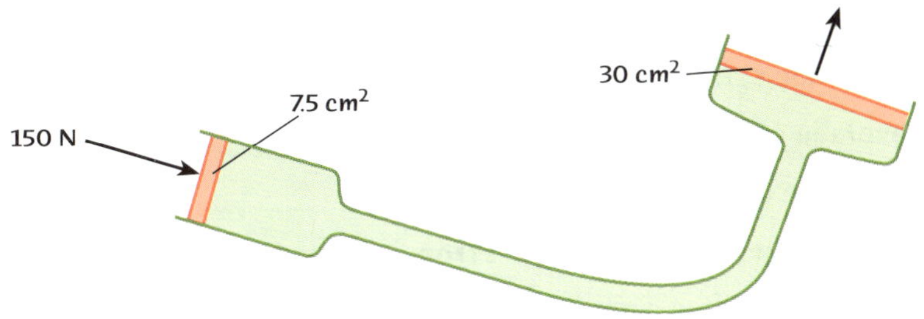

a Calculate the pressure on the hydraulic fluid. (3 marks)

b What pressure is exerted on the large piston? (1 mark)

c Calculate the force on the large piston. (2 marks)

d Some bicycles use hydraulic brakes rather than brakes operated by cables.
Give **two** advantages of hydraulic brakes. (2 marks)

3 A carbon dioxide gas cylinder has a volume of 120 cm^3.
It contains gas at a pressure of 1.25×10^6 Pa.

a Explain how the gas exerts a pressure. (2 marks)

b The valve is opened. The gas expands until its pressure is equal to atmospheric pressure (1.01×10^5 Pa).
Calculate the new volume of the gas. (3 marks)

c Suggest why the volume of gas that leaves the cylinder is less than the answer to b. (1 mark)

Revision Unit 20

Force and motion

The Check Up

1 Write down the formula for calculating the average speed of a moving object. ______

2 How long does it take to travel 1.2 m at an average speed of 0.5 m/s? ______

3 What does the slope or gradient of a distance–time graph represent? ______

4 What extra information is needed to describe an object's velocity, apart from its speed? ______

5 If an object has a negative velocity, what does the negative sign mean? ______

6 Write down the formula for calculating acceleration. ______

7 What is the unit of acceleration? ______

8 What feature of a velocity–time graph represents acceleration? ______

9 Describe what is meant by *thinking distance*. ______

______

10 Describe what is meant by *braking distance*. ______

______

11 What is the relationship between *thinking distance*, *braking distance* and *stopping distance*?

______

12 A vehicle travels at 25 m/s along a level road. The driving force is 2500 N. What is the size of the resistive force, and in which direction does it act?

Refer to these diagrams when answering questions 13 and 14.

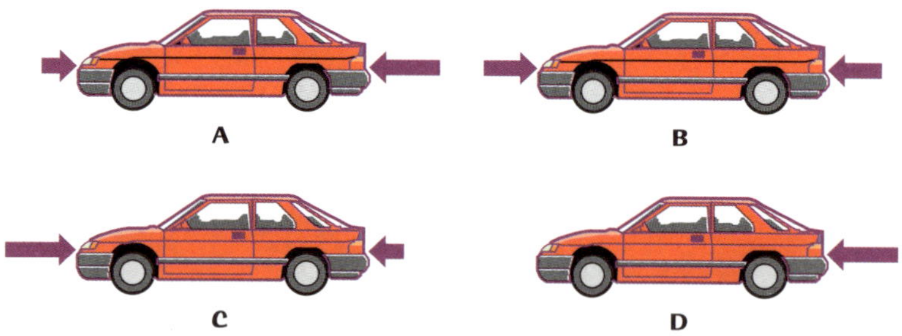

13 Which diagram shows a car that could be accelerating in the reverse direction? ______

14 Which diagram shows a car that could be travelling at a constant speed? ______

This graph shows how the speed of a falling object changes with time. Refer to the graph when answering questions 15–17.

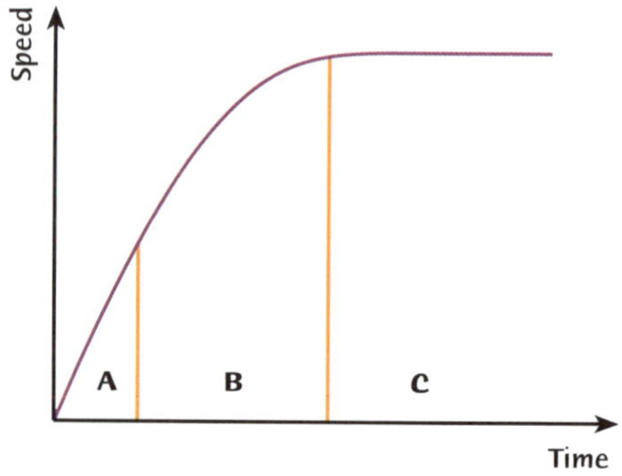

15 On which section of the graph is the object travelling at terminal velocity? ______

16 On which section of the graph does the object have the greatest acceleration? ______

17 On which section of the graph are the forces acting on the object balanced? ______

Continued ▶

The Check Up

18 Write down the relationship between the size of the unbalanced force acting on an object, its mass and its acceleration. ______

19 What **two** forces act on a falling object? State the direction of each force.

______

20 Calculate the weight of a 65 kg person. ($g = 10$ N/kg) ______

Mark yourself *(see answers on page 118)*

- More than 12? Do the exam practice – or go onto another unit.
- Less than 12? Do the crash course below.

/20

The Crash Course

Speed and velocity

The average speed of an object is calculated using:

average speed = distance travelled ÷ time taken or $v = s \div t$

It can also be calculated as the **gradient** or **slope** of a **distance–time graph**. It is measured in m/s.

Velocity is the speed in a specified direction. Movement in that direction is a positive velocity. A negative value is given to movement in the opposite direction.

Starting and stopping

A change in velocity is an **acceleration**.

Acceleration is calculated using:

acceleration = increase in velocity ÷ time taken or $a = (v_2 - v_1) \div t$

It can also be calculated as the **gradient** of a velocity-time graph. It is measured in m/s^2.

The distance that a vehicle travels from when the driver sees a hazard to when it stops is the **stopping distance**. It is made up of the **thinking distance** and the **braking distance**.

Thinking distance is the distance the vehicle travels during the driver's **reaction time**. It is proportional to the speed of the vehicle.

Braking distance is the distance the vehicle travels during braking. It is proportional to the vehicle's $(\text{speed})^2$.

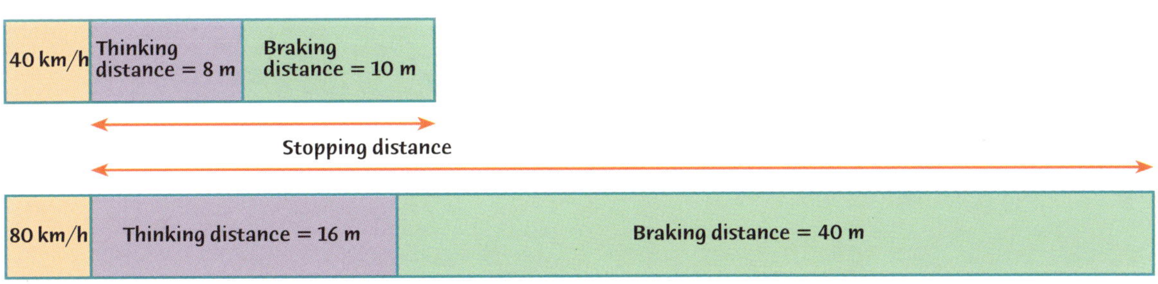

The Crash Course

Force and acceleration

If an object is not changing its velocity, the forces on it are **balanced**.

Unbalanced forces cause a change in velocity in the direction of the unbalanced force.

The relationship between the size of the unbalanced force and the acceleration it causes is:

force = mass x acceleration or $F = ma$

Falling down

Two forces act on a falling object. The object's **weight** (the Earth's pull) acts downwards and **resistive forces** (the push of the air) act upwards.

Close to the Earth's surface, the weight has a fixed value, given by:

weight = mass x gravitational field strength or $W = m \times g$*

The size of the resistive force depends on the object's speed and profile. The faster the object travels, the bigger the resistive force.

A falling object accelerates downwards if the weight is greater than the resistive force.

If the weight and resistive force are equal in size they are **balanced** and the object travels at a constant speed called **terminal velocity**.

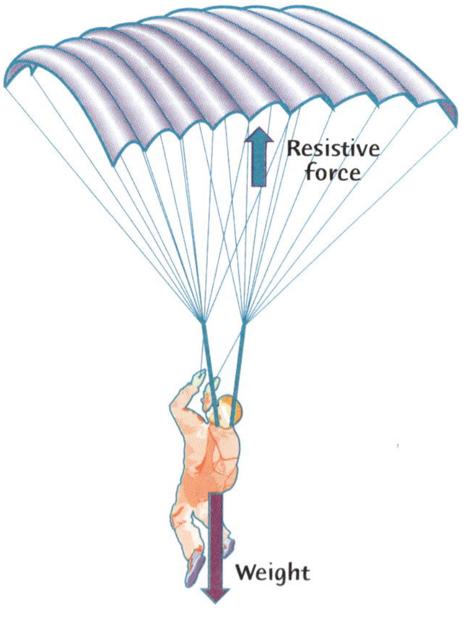

* this formula will be provided on examination papers

EXAM PRACTICE

1 The graph represents part of a car journey.

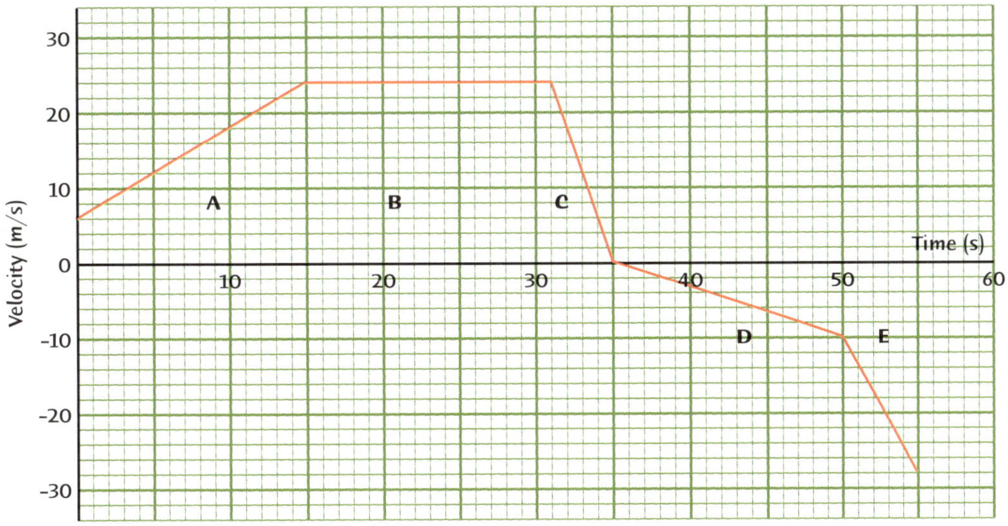

a How long did the car spend travelling at a constant speed? **1 mark**

b On which sections of the graph was the car increasing its speed? **2 marks**

c What is the greatest speed shown on the graph? **1 mark**

d What **two** changes to the motion of the car occurred after 35 s? **2 marks**

e Calculate the acceleration of the car during the first 15 s shown on the graph. **4 marks**

f Calculate the distance travelled by the car during section C of the graph. **3 marks**

2 A cycle and cyclist have a combined mass of 80 kg.
As the cyclist sets off, the resistive force is zero.

a Calculate the initial acceleration if the driving force is 120 N. **3 marks**

b Describe what happens to the size of the resistive force as the cyclist speeds up. **1 mark**

c Explain how this affects the acceleration of the cyclist. **2 marks**

d The driving force remains 120 N.
What is the size of the resistive force when the cyclist travels at a constant speed of 12 m/s? **1 mark**

e The cyclist notices a hazard and after 0.6 s she applies the brakes, coming to a halt 1.5 s later.

i) Calculate the cyclist's stopping distance. **4 marks**

ii) Explain how the stopping distance could be affected by wet weather. **1 mark**

Revision Unit 21

Waves

The Check Up

1 The frequency of a wave is the number of ______________________

2 Frequency is measured in ____________ .

3 Write down the formula that relates the speed of a wave to its frequency and wavelength.

____

4 Describe the difference between a longitudinal wave and a transverse wave.

____

5 Is sound longitudinal or transverse? ____________

6 What is ultrasound? ______________________

7 State one use of ultrasound. ______________________

8 Which wave property is shown by each of the following diagrams?

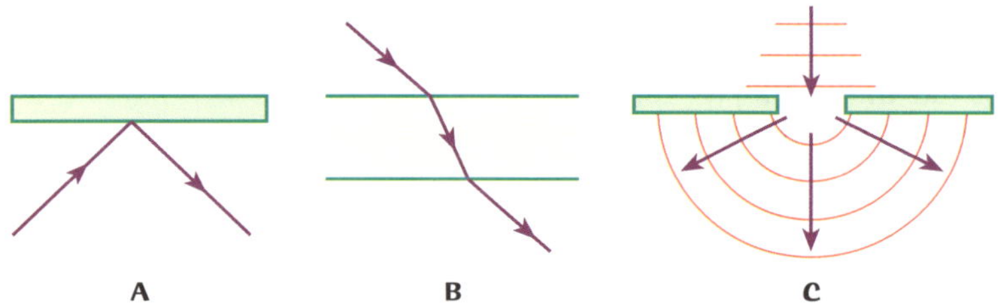

____

9 Which of the wave properties in question 8 is due to a change in speed? ____________

10 When waves spread out as they pass through a gap, what **two** factors does the amount of spreading depend on? ______________________

11 Are light waves longitudinal or transverse? ______________________

12 What does the amplitude of a wave measure? ______________________

13 When light meets a glass-air surface it can only pass through the surface if the angle of incidence is

______________________ .

14 If no light passes through the surface ____________ ____________ ____________ occurs.

15 Why is the spreading out of light at a gap difficult to observe? ____________

16 Which **two** types of electromagnetic wave can be used to cook food? ____________

17 Which electromagnetic waves have the longest wavelength? ____________

18 Why are gamma rays more hazardous to humans than radio waves are? ____________

19 What properties of X-rays make them suitable for examining fractures? ____________

20 Which waves have a wavelength shorter than that of light but longer than that of X-rays and gamma rays?

____

Mark yourself *(see answers on page 119)*

- More than 12? Do the exam practice – or go onto another unit.
- Less than 12? Do the crash course on the next page.

/ 20

THE CRASH COURSE

Wave properties

Waves transfer energy without any transfer of material.

The **frequency** (*f*) of a wave is the number of cycles of the wave that occur each second. It is measured in hertz (Hz).

The **wavelength** (λ) of a wave is the length of one cycle.

The **amplitude** of a wave is the greatest displacement from the normal position.

The **speed** (*v*) of a wave is related to its wavelength and frequency by the formula:

speed = frequency × wavelength $v = f \times \lambda$

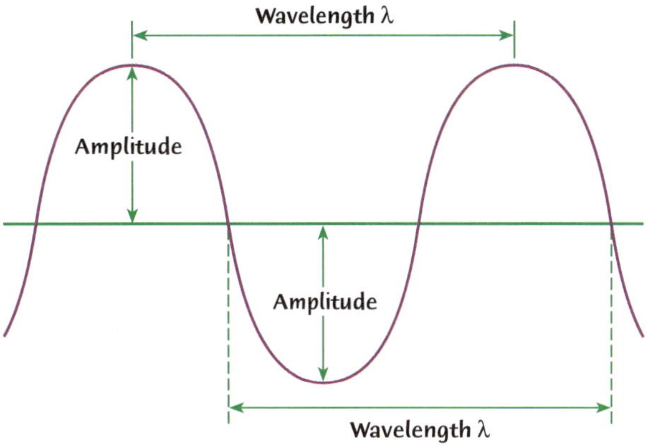

A transverse wave

Sound and ultrasound

Sound waves are **longitudinal**; the vibrations are parallel to the direction of travel of the wave.

Increasing the frequency of a sound causes an increase in **pitch**.

Increasing the amplitude of a sound causes an increase in **loudness**.

A reflection of a sound is called an **echo**.

Ultrasound has a frequency above the range of human hearing. Reflections of ultrasound are used to measure distances and build up images of body organs.

Sound changes speed when it passes through materials of different density. This is called **refraction**. The change in speed may also cause a change in direction.

Sound waves are readily **diffracted**. They spread out when they pass through a gap. The amount of spreading depends on the size of the gap compared to the wavelength.

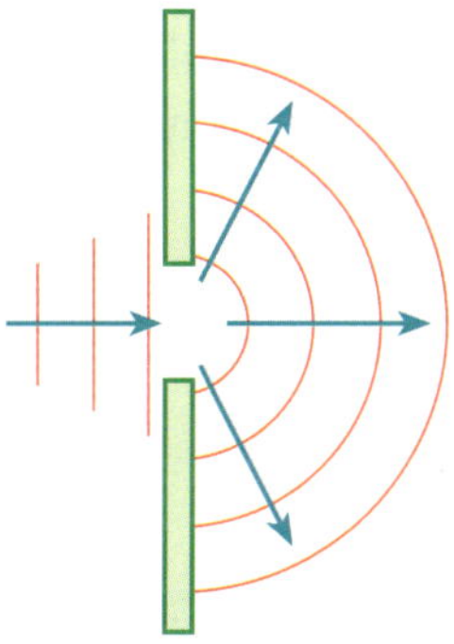

Diffraction of a wave as it passes through a gap

Light

Light and other electromagnetic waves are **transverse**; the vibrations are at right angles to the direction of wave travel.

Non-luminous objects are seen by the light that they scatter (reflect in all directions). Mirrors reflect light at equal angles, forming **virtual images**.

Virtual images are also formed by the **refraction** of light, the change in speed which may be accompanied by a change in direction when light passes through materials of different density.

Light striking a glass-air surface at an angle above the **critical angle** is **totally internally reflected**. This is used in reflecting prisms and optical fibres.

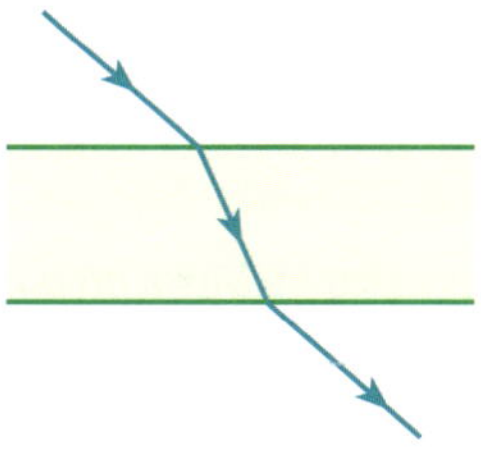

The change in direction when light is refracted by glass

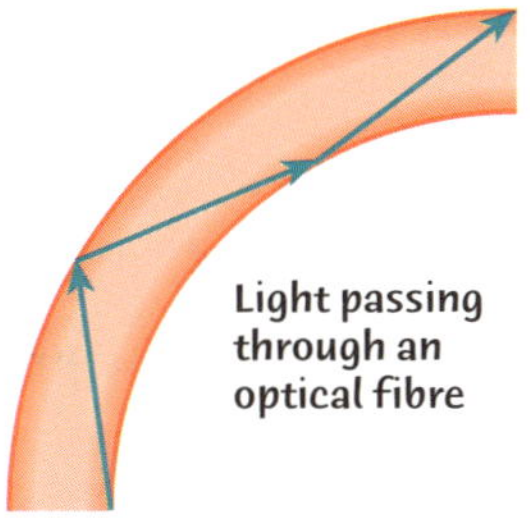

Light passing through an optical fibre

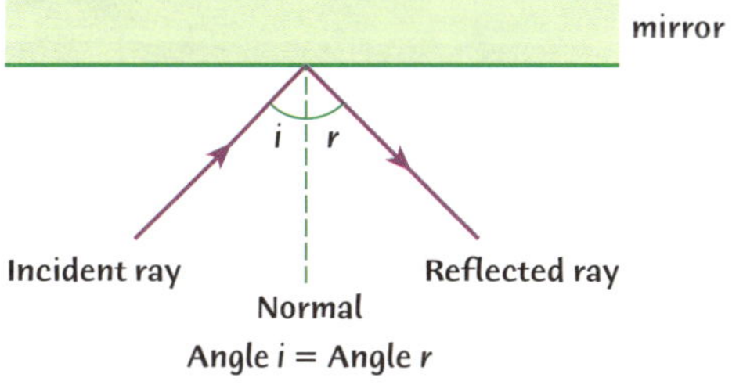

Reflection of light rays by a mirror

THE CRASH COURSE

The electromagnetic spectrum

The diagram below shows the approximate wavelengths and frequencies of electromagnetic waves.

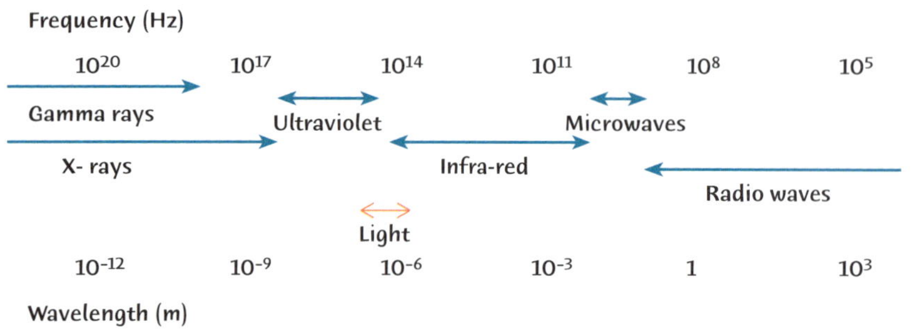

Radio waves, microwaves and infra-red waves have a longer wavelength and lower frequency than light. Radio waves and microwaves are readily diffracted because of their longer wavelength.

X-rays, gamma rays and ultraviolet waves have a shorter wavelength and higher frequency than light. They are more penetrative and can damage human tissue.

EXAM PRACTICE

1 Ultrasound is used to measure the depth of a lake.
The speed of ultrasound in water is 1500 m/s.
The frequency of the waves used is 50 000 Hz.

a Calculate the wavelength of the ultrasound. **3 marks**

b A pulse of waves is sent out and the echo arrives back 0.30 s later.
Calculate the depth of the lake. **3 marks**

c The boat carrying out the test passes over a shoal of fish swimming close to the surface.
Explain how this affects the time it takes for the echo to return. **2 marks**

2 a The diagram shows light passing through a reflecting prism.

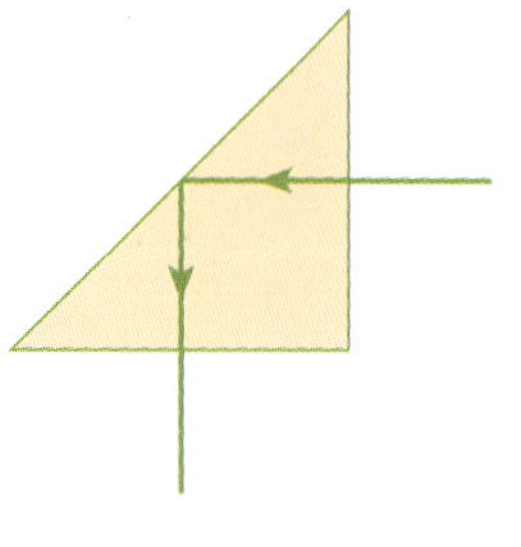

i) What is the condition for all the light to be reflected at the inside face of the prism? **3 marks**

ii) State one use of a reflecting prism. **1 mark**

Continued ▶

EXAM PRACTICE

b Surgeons use endoscopy to see inside the body.
The diagram shows an optical fibre being used to light up the stomach.

i) Draw a diagram that shows how light travels along the fibre. **2 marks**

ii) Suggest how a surgeon is able to see light reflected from inside the stomach. **1 mark**

iii) Suggest one advantage of using optical fibres rather than X-rays to 'see' inside the body. **1 mark**

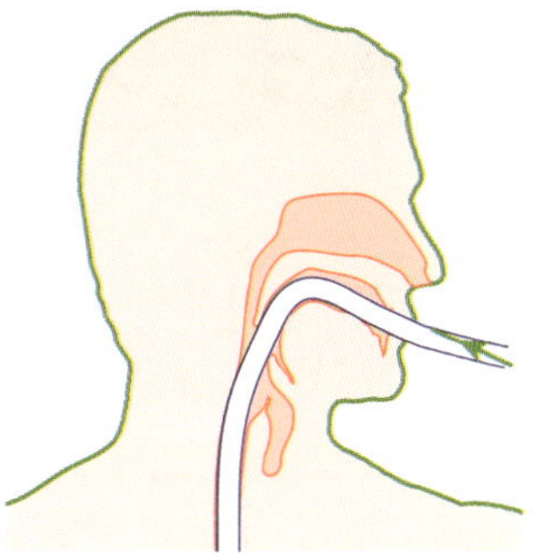

3 VHF radio waves have a wavelength of around 3.00 m.
They travel in air at a speed of 3.00×10^8 m/s.

a Calculate the frequency of a VHF radio wave. **3 marks**

Radio 4 is broadcast both on VHF and long wave, at a wavelength of 1500 m.

The diagram shows how tall buildings can prevent the reception of VHF waves but not that of long waves.

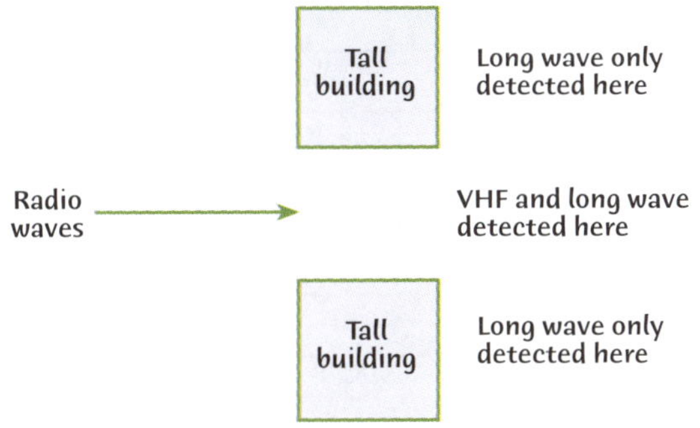

b Explain why the long wave broadcast can be detected in the 'shadow' but the VHF broadcast cannot be. **4 marks**

c 'Light travels in straight lines but sound can travel round obstacles.' Explain why. **2 marks**

Revision Unit 22

The Earth and beyond

The Check Up

1 How many stars are there in the Solar System? ____________

2 Give **two** reasons why Mercury takes the shortest time of all the planets to complete an orbit of the Sun.

____

3 Which type of wave, longitudinal or transverse, cannot pass through the outer core of the Earth?

____

4 How is the outer core thought to be different from the inner core? ____________

5 The Sun's gravitational pull on Mercury is *less than/equal to/greater than* Mercury's pull on the Sun.

____

6 Explain why the inner planets are warmer than the outer planets.

____

7 What lies between the inner planets and the outer planets? ____________

8 At which planet is the Sun's gravitational field strength at its weakest? ____________

9 Suggest why the size of the Sun's pull on Jupiter is greater than that on the Earth.

____

10 Give **two** uses of artificial satellites. ____________

11 What causes the glow when a comet passes close to the Sun?

____

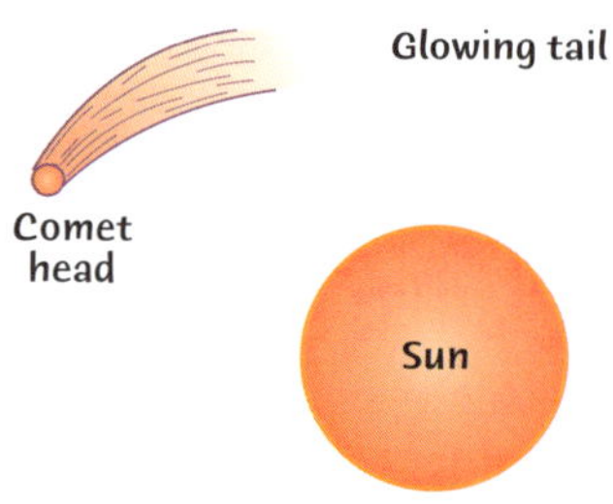

12 At which point on a comet's orbit is the Sun's gravitational pull at its strongest?

____

13 Give **two** differences between the orbit of a comet and that of a planet.

____

14 What type of force can cause part of a dust cloud to collapse and form a star?

____

15 What happens to the temperature of a star as it expands? ____________

16 Place the following stages in the life of a small star in the correct order:

red supergiant   main sequence   white dwarf

____

17 The diagram represents the movement of the galaxies. What does this suggest about the origin of the Universe?

____

18 What is a supernova? ____________

19 What happens to a star after it becomes a supernova? ____________

20 What name is given to the theory that the Universe started with an enormous explosion? ____________

Mark yourself *(see answers on page 120)*

- More than 12? Do the exam practice – or go onto another unit.
- Less than 12? Do the crash course on the next page.

/20

The Crash Course

The Earth's structure

The Earth consists of several layers: thin outer **crust**, **mantle** and **core**.

At the centre of the Earth is the solid inner core surrounded by the liquid outer core.

Evidence for the liquid outer core comes from the passage of **longitudinal** and **transverse** waves through the Earth.

Longitudinal waves pass through all parts of the Earth, but transverse waves form a **shadow**. As transverse waves do not pass through the body of a liquid, this shows that part of the inner Earth must be liquid.

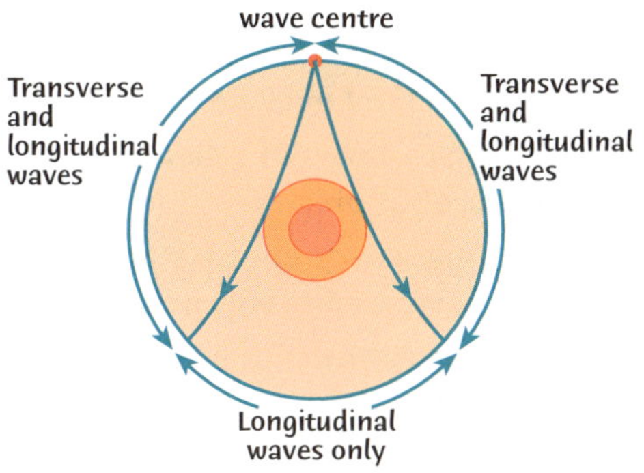

The planets

Mercury, Venus, Earth and Mars are the inner, rocky planets. Mercury and Venus are the only planets with no moons.

The inner planets are separated from the outer planets by the **asteroid belt**.

Jupiter, Saturn, Uranus, Neptune and Pluto are the outer planets. They are cold and are composed largely of gases and ice.

Movement through space

Movement of planets, moons, satellites and comets is determined by **gravitational attractive forces**.

The attractive forces between any two objects are **equal in size** and act in **opposite directions**.

The **gravitational field strength** of the Sun, and any other object, becomes weaker with increasing distance from it.

Most planets follow mainly circular **orbits**, so the attractive force has a constant value but changes in direction.

Comets consist mainly of frozen water and gases; they orbit the Sun in elliptical orbits in any direction, the attractive force becoming less as they move further away from the Sun.

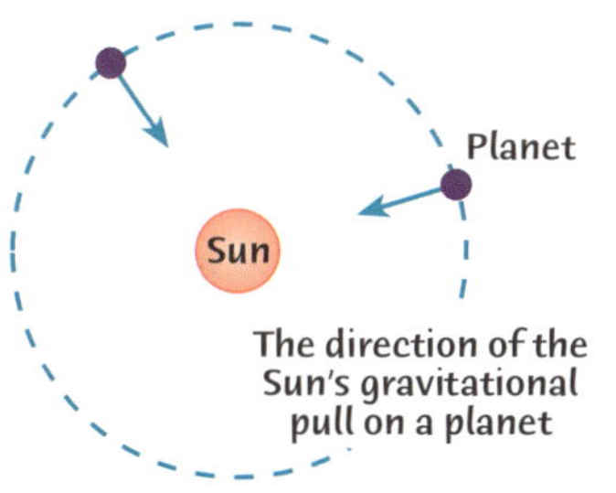

The universe

The universe is thought to have begun with a massive explosion, called the 'big bang'. It has been expanding and cooling ever since.

If the movement of the galaxies is plotted, they all seem to have started from a single point.

The universe may continue to expand and cool, or it may contract and heat. A third possibility is that it will reach a steady size.

The Crash Course

Stars

Stars are created in clouds of dust and hydrogen gas.

The collapse of part of a cloud due to gravitational forces makes a region of very dense material which gives off energy due to **nuclear fusion**.

After its **main sequence** a star expands to a **red supergiant**. A small star then collapses into a **white dwarf** and continues to cool.

Larger stars contract to become **blue supergiants** before expanding again into red supergiants.

A further contraction can create a **supernova**, which explodes to form a **neutron star** and a dust cloud.

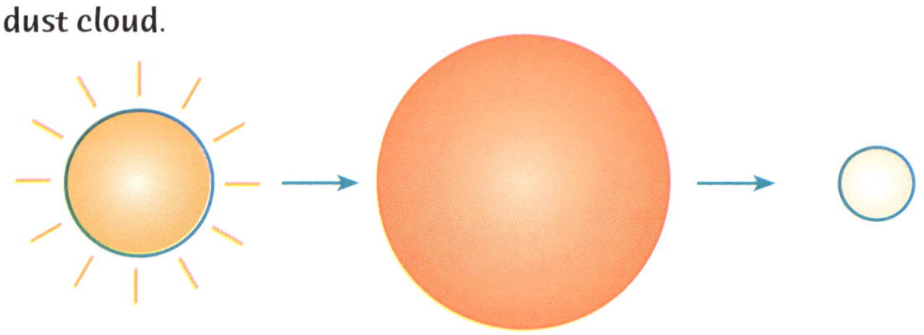

Stages in the life cycle of a small star

Exam Practice

1 The table gives data about the five outer planets.

Planet	Mean distance from Sun compared to Earth	Mean orbital speed (km/s)	Time to rotate once on own axis (h)	Surface gravitational field strength (N/kg)
Jupiter	5.2	13.1	10	23.0
Saturn	9.5	9.6	11	9.0
Uranus	19.1		17	8.7
Neptune	30.0	5.4	16	11.0
Pluto	39.5	4.7	150	0.7

a i) On which planet would a 1 kg mass weigh the most? **1 mark**

ii) Which planet would be easiest to escape from? **1 mark**

b Which planet has the shortest day? **1 mark**

c i) Which planet has the longest year? **1 mark**

ii) Give **two** reasons why this planet has the longest year. **2 marks**

d i) Use the data to plot a graph of mean orbital speed (y axis) against mean distance from the Sun (x axis). **4 marks**

ii) What is the relationship between the distance from the Sun and the mean orbital speed? **1 mark**

iii) Suggest a reason for this. **1 mark**

iv) Use your graph to estimate the mean orbital speed of Uranus. **1 mark**

Continued

Exam Practice

2 Mercury goes round the Sun in an elliptical orbit.

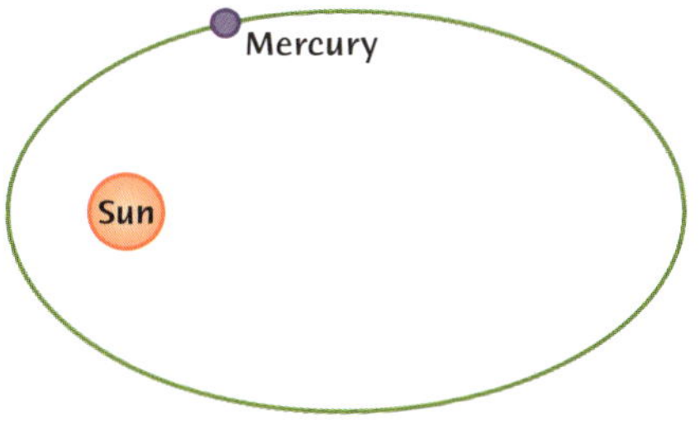

a Describe how the gravitational force on Mercury changes during one complete orbit. **3 marks**

b How does Mercury's pull on the Sun compare to the Sun's pull on Mercury? **2 marks**

c Mercury has very long days and nights.
Suggest how this affects the temperature on the surface of Mercury. **2 marks**

3 Our Sun is thought to have formed from the remains of an exploding supernova.

a Suggest how this could have happened. **3 marks**

b At the end of its main sequence our Sun will start to cool.
Describe what is likely to happen next. **2 marks**

Revision Unit 23

Energy

The Check Up

1 Hot objects can lose energy by conduction, convection, radiation and ______

2 Which method involves movement of a fluid owing to changes in density? ______

3 Which method can transfer energy through a vacuum? ______

4 Which method involves particles leaving the surface of a liquid? ______

5 Which type of surface is the best **emitter** of radiant energy? ______

6 Which type of surface is the best **absorber** of radiant energy? ______

The diagram shows a hot potato insulated with bubble-wrap.

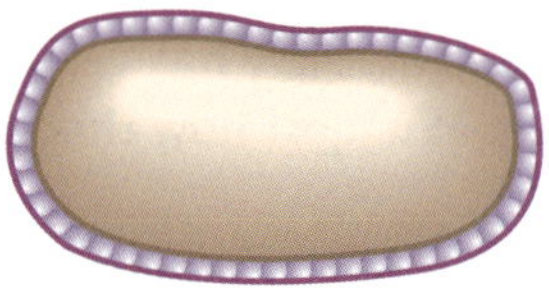

Insulated hot potato

7 How is the bubble-wrap effective in reducing energy loss by conduction?

______

8 How is the bubble-wrap effective at reducing energy loss by convection?

______

9 Give **two** reasons why aluminium foil is a good insulator for a hot take-away meal. ______

______

10 Hot air rising from a central heating radiator is an example of ______

11 Why is wood described as being a renewable energy source? ______

______

12 Name **two** non-renewable energy sources that are fossil fuels. ______

13 "The efficiency of a coal-burning power station is 38%." What does this statement mean?

______

14 Why is it necessary to develop power stations that are more efficient?

______

For questions 15–18

A 40 kg child climbs to the top of the slide shown in the diagram.
($g = 10\ m/s^2$)

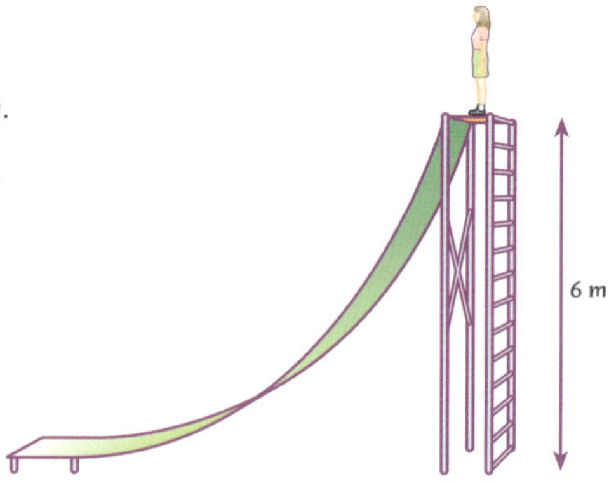

15 Calculate the child's gravitational potential energy at the top of the slide. ______

16 What energy transfer takes place as the child travels down the slide? ______

17 Suggest how this energy transfer could be made more efficient. ______

______

18 The child is travelling at 7 m/s at the bottom of the slide. Calculate the child's kinetic energy.

______

Continued ▶

The Check Up

For questions 19 and 20

A person uses a 45 N force to push a vacuum cleaner 8 m horizontally.

19 How much work does the person do? ____________________

20 How much energy is transferred from the person? ____________________

Mark yourself *(see answers on page 120)*

- More than 12? Do the exam practice – or go onto another unit.
- Less than 12? Do the crash course below.

/20

The Crash Course

Energy transfer

The mechanisms by which energy is transferred between objects at different temperatures are **conduction**, **convection**, **radiation** and **evaporation**.

Conduction takes place in all materials and involves energy transfer from more energetic particles to less energetic ones.

Convection only takes place in fluids (liquids and gases). Warmer, less dense fluid, rises and colder, denser fluid sinks.

All objects emit **electromagnetic radiation**. For objects at everyday temperatures this is mainly infra-red radiation. Dark surfaces are better than light surfaces at emitting and absorbing radiant energy.

Evaporation takes place from the surface of a liquid. It causes the remaining liquid to cool.

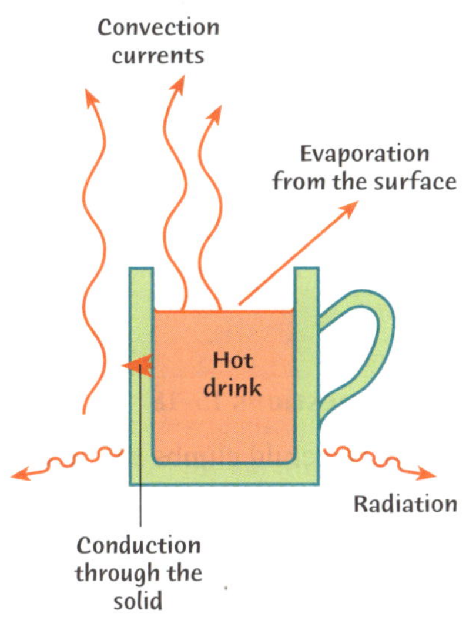

Heat loss from a hot drink

Insulation

Insulation with trapped air pockets is effective in reducing energy transfer by conduction and convection.

Shiny surfaces such as aluminium foil reduce energy losses through radiation.

Evaporation of a liquid can ususally be reduced by keeping it covered.

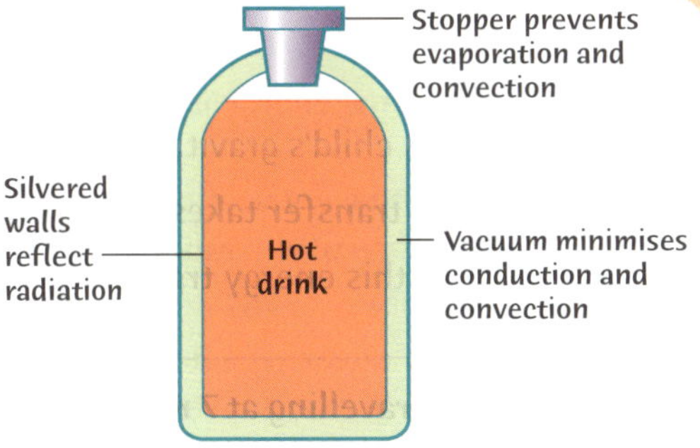

Reducing heat loss in a vacuum flask

THE CRASH COURSE

Energy sources and efficiency

Fossil fuels such as **coal**, **oil** and North Sea **gas** (methane) are **non-renewable**; they cannot be replaced within the lifetime of the Earth.

Wood, wind, and energy from moving water are all **renewable** sources of energy.

The **efficiency** of an energy transfer is the fraction or percentage of energy from the source that is transferred to where it is needed.

Energy and work

All movement involves an energy transfer, known as doing **work**.

The energy transfer or work done is calculated using the formula:

work done = force x distance moved in direction of force $W = F \times d$

Energy and work are measured in joules (J).

Power is the rate of working or energy transfer:

Power = work done or energy transfer ÷ time taken $P = W \div t$*

Power is measured in watts (W).

A moving object has **kinetic energy**,

kinetic energy $= \frac{1}{2} \times \text{mass} \times (\text{velocity})^2$ $ke = \frac{1}{2} \times m \times v^2$*

An object that is rising or falling is changing its **gravitational potential energy**.

gravitational potential energy = weight × height = mass × g × height $GPE = m \times g \times h$*

* these formulae will be provided on examination papers

EXAM PRACTICE

1 a The diagram shows how **conduction**, **convection** and **radiation** are all involved in transferring energy from a hot radiator to a cooler room.

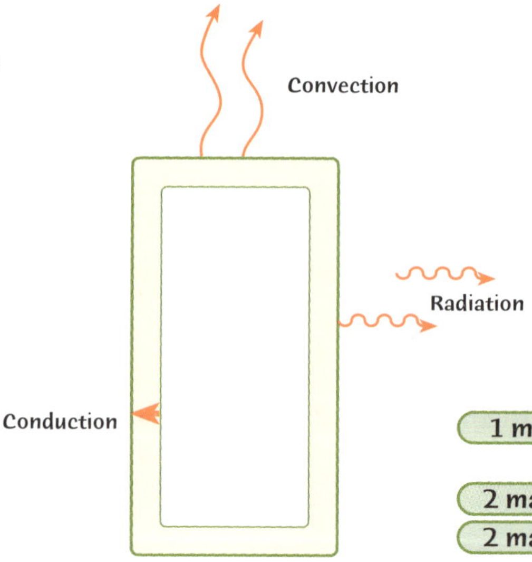

i) Explain how energy is conducted through the metal radiator. **1 mark**

ii) Explain how convection currents remove energy from the surface of the radiator. **2 marks**

iii) Explain how energy is radiated from the surface. **2 marks**

b Explain why covering a hot drink with a lid is one of the most effective ways of reducing the rate of cooling. **2 marks**

Continued ▶

Exam Practice

2 Wind farms generate electricity from moving air.

a Suggest **three** advantages of building wind farms. (3 marks)

b There is often opposition to building new wind farms. Suggest **three** reasons why. (3 marks)

3 A car pulls a caravan with a 600 N force for a distance of 150 m.

a Calculate the work done by the car in pulling the caravan. (3 marks)

b It takes 20 s to travel 150 m.
Calculate the power of the car used to tow the caravan. (3 marks)

c The caravan reaches a speed of 15 m/s. The mass of the caravan is 450 kg.
Calculate the kinetic energy of the caravan. (3 marks)

d How efficient is the transfer of energy from the car to the caravan? (2 marks)

e Suggest where the rest of the energy goes to. (1 mark)

Revision Unit 24

Radioactivity

The Check Up

1 Name **three** natural sources of background radiation.

2 Name **two** ways in which human activity contributes to the background radiation.

3 Which part of an atom emits radioactivity?

4 Why is it important to take an average reading when measuring background radiation?

Questions 5–11

Which type of radioactive emission:

5 Is negatively charged?

6 Has the greatest mass?

7 Is most easily stopped?

8 Can penetrate paper but not lead?

9 Is the most intensely ionising?

10 Consists of short wavelength electromagnetic radiation?

11 Causes no change to the atomic number or mass number of the nucleus that emits it?

12 Explain why a gamma-emitter is more suitable than an alpha or beta-emitter for tracing a leak in an underground pipe, as shown in the diagram.

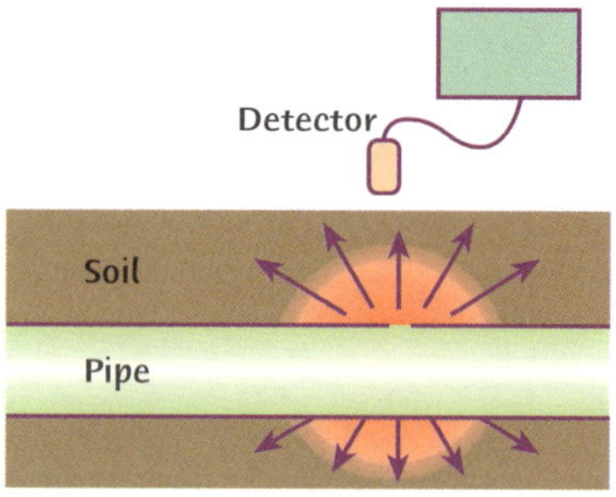

Tracing a leak from a pipe

13 What is the meaning of the term "half-life"?

14 A radioactive sample contains 10 g of technetium-99, a gamma-emitter that has a half-life of 6 hours. How much technetium-99 remains in the sample 12 hours later?

15 Domestic smoke alarms use alpha-emitters. Explain why these are not dangerous to people standing near them.

16 Why is alpha radiation the most dangerous when inside the human body?

17 Name a suitable detector of ionising radiation.

Continued ▶

The Check Up

18 Explain why a beta-emitter is more suitable than an alpha-emitter for monitoring the thickness of aluminium foil, as shown in the diagram. ______

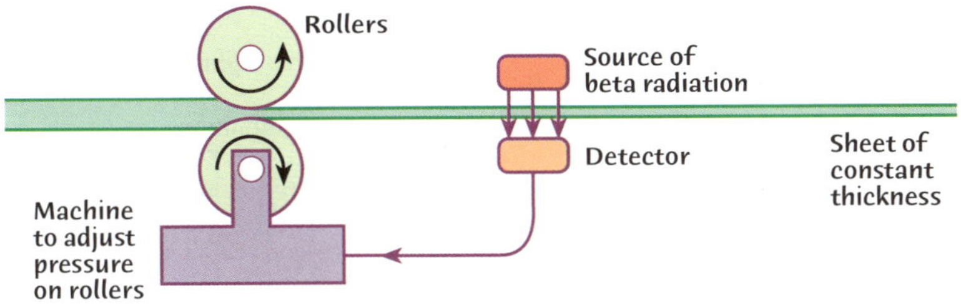

Carbon-14 is a radioactive isotope that exists in all objects that are alive or have been alive. Its half-life is 6000 years.

19 What proportion of the original carbon-14 would you expect to find in a wooden beam thought to be 24 000 years old? ______

20 Why can carbon-14 not be used to estimate the age of Moon rock? ______

Mark yourself *(see answers on page 121)*

- More than 12? Do the exam practice – or go onto another unit.
- Less than 12? Do the crash course below.

/20

The Crash Course

Origins of radioactivity

Ionising **radiation** is given off by the food we eat, the air we breathe and the Earth that we live on. We are continually being bombarded by radiation from the Sun and space. All this radiation is known as "**background radioactivity**".

Nuclear power, nuclear weapons and medical uses of radioactivity also contribute to the **background radiation**.

Radioactive emissions are given off when an unstable nucleus changes to a more stable form.

All radioactive emissions are random events; they cannot be predicted.

The Crash Course

Types of emission

The three main types of emission are known as alpha (α), beta (β) and gamma (γ).

Alpha radiation is the least penetrative, being absorbed by thin paper or a few centimetres of air. It is intensely ionising. It is positively charged, each alpha particle consisting of two protons and two neutrons.

Beta radiation can penetrate a thickness of several millimetres thickness of aluminium. It is less ionising than alpha radiation and is negatively charged, consisting of fast-moving electrons.

Gamma radiation is the most penetrative and least ionising of the three. Its intensity can be reduced by a thickness of several centimetres of lead. It consists of very short wavelength electromagnetic radiation.

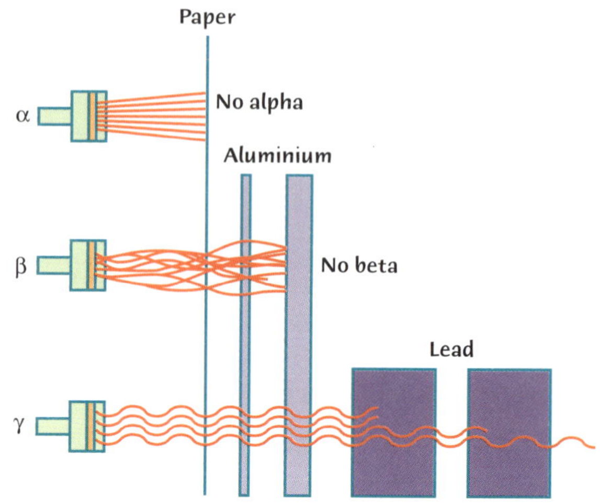

The table shows the effect on the remaining nucleus when alpha, beta or gamma radiation is emitted.

Emission	Effect on atomic number	Effect on mass number
alpha	−2	−4
beta	+1	0
gamma	0	0

Half-life

The average time take for the number of undecayed nuclei in a sample of material to halve is known as the **half-life** of the material. It is often measured as the time taken for the decay rate of a sample to halve.

Materials with short half-lives decay more rapidly than those with long half-lives.

Using the emissions

Alpha and beta emitters are both used to measure and monitor the thickness of sheet materials.

Gamma emitters are used as tracers because of their higher penetrative power.

All types of radiation can cause cell damage and cancer when absorbed by body tissue. They can also be used to treat cancers.

Once-living things can be dated by measuring the amount of radioactive carbon-14 that they contain.

Rocks can be dated by comparing the amounts of radioactive material and the product formed when it decays.

EXAM PRACTICE

1 The emissions from a sample of polonium-214 are recorded for periods of ten seconds at one minute intervals.
The results are shown in the table.

Time (min)	0	1	2	3	4	5	6	7	8
Number of counts in 10 s	4500	3683	3060	2498	2025	1710	1388	1110	908
Activity (counts/s)									

a i) Complete the third row of the table. 1 mark
ii) Suggest why the emissions are measured over a ten second period rather than just one second. 2 marks

b i) Apart from the polonium, what else could contribute to the measured activity? 1 mark
ii) Suggest how the readings could be corrected for this. 2 marks

c i) Use the data in the table to plot a graph of activity (y-axis) against time (x-axis). 4 marks
ii) Use your graph to work out a value for the half-life of polonium. 3 marks

d i) Describe how the decay of the polonium changes over the 8 min represented by the graph. 1 mark
ii) Suggest why it changes in this way. 1 mark

2 a Technetium-99 is a *radioactive* tracer used in medicine.
It emits *gamma radiation* only and decays with a *half-life* of six hours.
Explain the meaning of each term in *italics*. 6 marks

b Technetium-99 is injected into the bloodstream. It circulates through the body organs.
It can then be detected outside the body.
i) Name a suitable detector. 1 mark
ii) Why is it important for this purpose that the tracer used emits gamma radiation? 1 mark
iii) Why is it an advantage that the tracer used does not emit alpha or beta radiation? 2 marks

ANSWERS

Unit 1

The Check Up

1 The cell **2** Respiration Sensitivity Movement Excretion **3** Respiration **4** Nucleus Cytoplasm Cell membrane Mitochondria **5** Cellulose cell wall Chloroplasts Large vacuole **6** Tissue **7** Liver **8** E.g. alimentary canal (gut) Cardiovascular **9** Allows some particles to pass through and not others **10** Surface membrane or Vacuolar membrane **11** Randomly **12** Diffusion **13** No energy supply is needed **14** From cell A to cell B **15** A partially permeable membrane **16** Direction of the water concentration gradient, from high to low **17** a Diffusion/capillarity b Osmosis **18** When the water concentration in the two cells is the same **19** When they are moved against a concentration gradient **20** Respiration provides the energy necessary for active transport to take place

Exam Practice

1 a Cellulose cell wall Chloroplasts Large vacuole (3 marks)

b Cell **B**/sperm has a tail or flagellum which enables it to move (1 mark)

Cell **C**/motor neurone has an extended thread of cytoplasm/axon which enables it to communicate over a long distance (1 mark)

> *Questions of this type are quite straightforward but too often candidates fail to make it absolutely clear as to which part of the diagram or data they are referring. Here it is important to start your statement with the label or name of the cell.*

2 a The **cell sap** (in the cells of the potato chips) **contains water and solutes**

The cells (of the potato chips) are surrounded by **partially permeable membranes**

Tap water (may have some solutes in it but the) **water concentration is very high**

Therefore (the conditions necessary for) **osmosis** (to occur exist)

There will be a (steep) **water concentration gradient**

Water will **move into the chips**

and (inflate) the cells **making them stiff/turgid**

Whereas those chips not placed in water will **lose water** from their surfaces by **evaporation**.

As a result they will lose (turgor) and **become soft/flaccid**. (8 marks)

> *This is a very demanding question. You are being asked to use information provided in the question, which might be new to you, give a reasoned explanation and at the same time bring out the essential differences between the two situations.*
>
> *One mark is scored for each of the points in bold type, up to the maximum for the question. You would not be expected to provide an answer that relates to the marking scheme 'word for word'; suitable alternatives would be agreed. The examiner might like to see the words included in brackets but they would not be essential for the mark. Note the use of the words 'therefore', 'whereas' and 'as a result'. Answers to questions where you are asked to 'Explain the difference …' should include link words such as 'whereas', 'but in the case of …' and 'however in …'.*

b Because cooking kills the potato cells destroying the partial permeability of the cell membranes

Therefore osmosis can no longer take place (2 marks)

> *Make sure that you use link words such as 'because', 'due to', 'since' and 'therefore' when answering questions that start with the word 'Explain …'.*

3 a From high concentration to low concentration (1 mark)

b Calcium (1 mark)

c The external/soil concentration for potassium is 1.0 mM and the internal, cell sap concentration is 22.0 mM

Therefore potassium ions must be absorbed against the concentration gradient

Potassium ions are absorbed by active transport

Therefore respiratory energy will be required for this to take place (4 marks)

> *This question is very testing and requires a lot of information for four marks. It is not enough simply to describe the results. You should include specific data from the table and link statements with words such as 'therefore' or 'since'.*

d i) Calcium (1 mark)

ii) The percentage increase values for the three ions differ

The plant does not absorb all three with the same efficiency

The plant may be absorbing the ions selectively

The active transport mechanism may be different for different ions (3 marks)

> *This too is a demanding question. You must not be put off by questions that include data that you can't remember or may not have met. This type of question is challenging your ability to reason. Let the question give you help. Here you are getting a clue from part (i) – the values are different. The ability to think imaginatively and to handle novel data is one of the most distinguishing features of a Higher level candidate.*

Unit 2

The Check Up

1 Sun

2 $6CO_2$ (carbon dioxide) + $6H_2O$ (water) $\longrightarrow$ $C_6H_{12}O_6$ (glucose) + $6O_2$ (oxygen)

3 chlorophyll **4** Light Carbon dioxide concentration Temperature **5** Red and blue **6** Green **7** Nitrogen **8** Fats Vitamins Mineral salts **9** All the components to provide raw materials for growth and repair, health factors and sufficient energy for the individual concerned **10** **E C A B D** **11** Getting food into the alimentary canal **12** Amylase maltose **13** Stomach **14** Sterilises food Provides correct pH for enzymes **15** Emulsifies fats/Turns fats to fatty acids + glycerol **16** Duodenum/small intestine **17** Fatty acids and glycerol **18** Length Folding of inner wall Villi and microvilli **19** In blood capillaries **20** Branch of the lymphatic system

Exam Practice

1 a i) $6CO_2$

$C_6H_{12}O_6$ (2 marks)

Note that the question includes the words 'symbols' and 'balanced equation'. There are not many areas within Biology where you will be tested in this particular way but a Higher level Science candidate should be able to write balanced symbol equations. It would not be appropriate to complete this as a word equation.

ii) Light
Chlorophyll (2 marks)

b i) 450 nm Blue
675 nm Red (4 marks)

In this question you are given the information in the question. The marks are awarded for making the correct observations from the diagram and extracting the correct data from the table. Do not be put off by new data or information you have not met. Some questions are structured to test your ability to use data. The question will probably be structured in order to lead you through the thinking process. So try to think clearly and to take things one step at a time.

ii) Requires oxygen (1 mark)

You are unlikely to have met the term 'aerobic' in the context of photosynthesis. You are however likely to have met it in your studies of respiration. It is important that you transfer knowledge from all areas of Science and apply it where appropriate.

iii) At 450 nm and 675 nm there are peak numbers of bacteria
The bacteria used need oxygen, and will seek it out
Therefore there must be peak concentrations of oxygen
Photosynthesis produces oxygen as a waste
Therefore peak numbers of bacteria indicate peaks of photosynthesis/fewer bacteria will mean less photosynthesis
Therefore photosynthesis is most effective with blue and red light/least effective with green light
(5 marks)

This question is very testing and requires a lot of information for five marks. It is not enough simply to describe the results. You should include specific data from the table and the diagram and link statements with words such as 'therefore', 'because' or 'since'.

2 a (Starch) Mouth Amylase Maltose
(Maltose) Duodenum/small intestine Maltase Glucose
(6 marks)

The words 'Starch' and 'Maltose' are in brackets to indicate that you will not score a mark for them. However, you will need to state them in your answer at the point indicated for your answer to make sense. If you have time repeat this question for proteins and/or fats. You can make up your own marking scheme from the diagram in the Crash Course.

b Labels/notes should include:
Thin surface layer of cells/epithelium
Blood vessel bringing blood to the villus; blood carries low concentration of dissolved food substances
Blood vessel taking blood away from the villus; blood carries high concentration of dissolved food substances
Particularly high in glucose and amino acids
Blood capillary network provides large surface area
Glucose and amino acids diffuse into blood capillaries
Steep concentration gradient
Lacteal/branch of lymphatic system, carries fatty acids and glycerol (5 marks)

This question requires a lot of information for five marks but it is straightforward and depends on accurate recall of facts. You should note that for most of the marks you have to link 'structure' and 'function'.

Unit 3

The Check Up

1 Glucose/sugar Oxygen **2** Lactic acid
3 Glucose ⟶ Carbon dioxide + Ethanol + Energy
4 Bread making Wine making and brewing **5** Causes muscle fatigue **6** Continued respiration after the available oxygen has been used up means that an organism has to respire anaerobically; this leads to an 'oxygen debt' **7** Fat Protein Carbohydrate **8** Adenosine Triphosphate made during respiration Used as 'energy currency' **9** **A** trachea **B** left bronchus **C** bronchiole **D** air sac/alveolus **E** diaphragm **10** thin; moist; permeable to gases involved; large surface area; close to transport system **11** Surface of air sacs/surface of alveoli **12** pulmonary artery **13** Diffusion **14** Concentration high in blood, lower in lung air space **15** Continuous ventilation and blood circulation **16** Increase **17** To oxidise the lactic acid/repay 'oxygen debt' **18** In the brain **19** Changes in concentration of blood carbon dioxide and lactic acid/hydrogen ions **20** Nerve impulses

Exam Practice

1 a i) **A** oxygen **B** Carbon dioxide (2 marks)
ii) Adenosine triphosphate (ATP) (1 mark)
iii) More ATP produced OR more carbon dioxide OR more water (1 mark)

You should remember that different types of food contain different quantities of energy per gram. Fats have a very large number of carbon to hydrogen bonds and the oxidation of these leads to the production of ATP. One gram of fat oxidised by respiration produces more than twice as much ATP as the oxidation of 1 g of carbohydrate. More carbon to carbon bonds and carbon to hydrogen bonds will also affect the number of moles of carbon dioxide and water produced.

b Carbon dioxide is produced during anaerobic respiration
Carbon dioxide is trapped in the dough
Pockets of gas trapped cause the dough to rise
Bread produced has a lighter texture/is leavened
(4 marks)

c i) Anaerobic at the finish, whereas it would have been aerobic at the start (1 mark)

You are asked to comment on the difference, therefore it is important that you make a statement that includes reference to both elements in the comparison, here, 'finish' and 'start', linked by words such as 'but' or 'whereas'.

ii) Resting muscle will have an adequate supply of oxygen
Therefore it can respire aerobically

Strenuous muscle action (during the course of the 100 m sprint) will use up oxygen faster than it can be supplied
Therefore ATP for subsequent muscle activity will have to be supplied anaerobically
Consequently an oxygen debt will arise
Raised ventilation rate for a period after the race will supply the oxygen to repay the 'debt' (6 marks)

You are asked to give an explanation. Make sure that you link statements, with words such as 'therefore', because', 'as a result' and 'consequently'.

2 a **D E B C A** (4 marks)

Questions of this type are likely to be marked as follows:
D before E; E before B; B before C; C before A;
Therefore, e.g. D B C A E would score 3 marks because:
D before E (1)
B before C (1)
C before A (1)
E before B (0)

b Ribs and sternum move up and out
Diaphragm is lowered/contracts
Therefore the volume of the thorax is increased
As a result the pressure inside the lung air space is decreased
Therefore a pressure gradient exists between the (external) atmosphere and the (internal) lung air space
Consequently air moves into the lung air space to equalise the pressure (5 marks)

The question asks you to explain how the mechanics cause the air to move in. A simple description of the mechanics of breathing would not answer the question. The answer should include statements relating to 'cause' and 'effect', linked by words such as 'therefore', 'because', consequently' and 'as a result'.

c Carbon dioxide (1 mark)

Unit 4

The Check Up

1 Sight Hearing Balance Smell Taste Touch **2** They transform the energy of a stimulus into nerve impulses **3** A tissue, organ or gland that has an effect – it brings about a change, i.e. the response **4 A** cell body **B** axon **C** myelin sheath **5** A microscopic gap between the end of one nerve cell and the next, communicating nerve cell **6** A reflex action **7** Hormonal glands have no ducts **8** Pancreas **9** Stimulates liver cells to convert blood glucose into glycogen **10** Testosterone **11** Ovary **12** Oestrogen Progesterone **13** Maintenance of a balanced, internal steady state **14** Pancreas Liver **15** Kidney tubule or nephron **16** Antidiuretic hormone (ADH) **17** Increases or decreases insulation by trapping more or less air respectively **18** The dilation (widening) of blood vessels **19** Auxin **20** Rooting powder or selective weedkiller

Exam Practice

1 a **A** Sound **B** Chemical **C** Gravity/movement (3 marks)
b **D** (Inner) Ear (1 mark)

An examiner would prefer Higher level candidates to refer to the 'Inner' ear but it is unlikely that it would be a requirement for the mark.

c Rods
Cones
Rods are peripheral
Cones are concentrated around the fovea
Rods are sensitive to low light intensity and provide black and white vision
Cones provide detail and colour vision but only in high light intensity (6 marks)

Always read the question carefully. Note that this question demands that your description includes reference to two things – 'distribution' and 'function'.

2 Nerve impulses arrive at the end of the nerve cell
Impulses initiate the secretion of neurotransmitter into the synaptic gap
Neurotransmitter stimulates next nerve cell in the series
Impulses are initiated
An enzyme present in the synaptic gap breaks down the neurotransmitter
Switching off transmission (5 marks)

3 a **D E C B A** (4 marks)

Questions of this type are likely to be marked as follows:
D before E; E before C; C before B; B before A;
Therefore someone answering: D E B C A,
would score 3 marks: D before E; E before C; B before A;
*but **not** C before B*

b i) Brain ii) Spinal cord (2 marks)

You must remember that some reflexes are called cranial reflexes, e.g. blinking or, iris reflex, because the sensory neurones in the reflex arc travel to the brain where relay neurones transmit impulses to motor neurones. This contrasts with examples such as the knee jerk or withdrawal reflexes of the limbs where the relay neurones are found in the grey matter of the spinal cord. This is why reference to reflexes as 'nerve pathways that do not involve the brain' are inadequate.

4 a Kidney tubules (1 mark)
b i) Increases the permeability of their membranes (1 mark)
ii) Less water is lost from the plasma (as a component of urine)/more water is retained (1 mark)
iii) Less ADH secreted (1 mark)

This question is straightforward but demands a clear understanding of the feedback mechanism involved in the kidney's role in water balance.

Unit 5

The Check Up

1 Links the heart to the lungs **2** Vena cava **3** Pressure of blood in the right atrium **4** Thicker muscle in the left ventricle **5** Aorta **6** Artery Thick muscular wall Small bore **7** Wall only one cell thick or gaps between adjacent cells **8** Two from: hormones, digestion products, enzymes, urea, mineral salts or named examples **9** Two from: Ingest bacteria or phagocytosis Secrete antibodies Remove cell debris **10** Red blood cell **11** Made in bone marrow from broken down dead red cells

12 Larger surface area for the exchange of oxygen **13** Wherever oxygen is required **14 A** Phloem **B** Xylem **15** Lignin **16** Conduction **17** Sucrose **18** By osmosis **19** Stomata **20** Reduce or lower the rate of transpiration

Exam Practice

1 a i) **A** pulmonary artery **B** pulmonary vein (2 marks)
ii) Blood in **B** will have: more oxygen; less carbon dioxide (2 marks)

Answers to questions that ask you to comment on differences must contain either comparatives such as 'more' or 'less', or statements linked by words such as 'whereas' or 'on the other hand'.

iii) The concentration of carbon dioxide in blood **A** will be higher than that in the alveoli therefore carbon dioxide will diffuse from the blood into the alveoli
The concentration of oxygen in the alveoli will be higher than that in blood **A** therefore oxygen will diffuse from the alveoli into the blood (2 marks)

It is important to use words such as 'therefore' or 'because' in answers to questions demanding explanation.

b Systemic circuit (1 mark)
c i) Pressure in C will be higher than that in **A** (1 mark)
ii) The wall of the left ventricle is more muscular than the wall of the right ventricle
therefore it will generate a higher blood pressure (2 marks)

The comment for a iii) applies here too.

2

left atrium:	collects blood from pulmonary vein
bicuspid valve:	prevents backflow of blood from ventricle
left ventricle:	muscular wall to pump blood out of the heart
pocket valves:	prevent backflow of blood from the aorta (8 marks)

It is always important to read questions carefully before you start to write your answer. Here it would be easy to take in the first part of the question and only gain half of the marks. You are being asked to do two things here – recall the sequence of structures and at the same time relate structure to function. You may find it helpful, when answering questions where sequence matters, to list the items to be sequenced in the margin of your paper and put them into order at that point. It is extremely difficult, in the limited space you are likely to be given, to rearrange things once you have started to write your answer.

3 a Osmosis (1 mark)
b Water molecules diffuse into the atmosphere
because there is a diffusion gradient from the leaf air spaces to the air
the water evaporates
from the damp cell walls of parenchyma cells in the leaf into the relatively 'drier' air spaces in the leaf
as a result the water content or water potential of the parenchyma cells is lowered
consequently water is pulled from the xylem in the leaf and in turn from xylem in the stem (6 marks)

This is a demanding question. Your answer must not only offer an explanation, but one where sequence is important. Therefore, as for question 2 above, a little time spent planning is likely to be rewarded by a better answer.

Unit 6

The Check Up

1 Mitosis **2** Two from: bulb, corm, stem tuber or rhizome **3** They are all genetically identical therefore all of them will be affected by the change **4** Fusion of two dissimilar nuclei or gametes or sex cells **5** A complete set of single chromosomes **6** i) Testes; ii) Ovaries **7** Vas deferens or sperm duct **8** Cowper's Prostate Seminal vesicles **9** Oviduct or Fallopian tube **10** Oviduct **11** Zygote **12** To produce pollen **13 A** anther **B** filament **C** stigma **D** style **E** ovary **14** Transfer of pollen from an anther to a receptive stigma **15** Two from: insects, wind, water, birds, bats or monkeys **16** E.g. insect-pollinated: coloured petals whereas wind-pollinated: inconspicuous or dull petals **17** Pollen tube grows down through style **18** A seed **19** Ovary wall or pericarp **20** Wall becomes fleshy and edible

Exam Practice

1 a **A** testis **B** vas deferens/sperm duct **C** urethra **D** oviduct/fallopian tube **E** uterus **F** vagina (6 marks)
b **A** (1 mark)
c **D** (1 mark)

If you have time, see whether you could offer a correct function for the other parts labelled on the diagrams.

2 **A** Large and colourful
B Small and inconspicuous
C Have short filaments
D Have long filaments
E Contained within the flower
F Hang outside the flower
G Contained within the flower
H Net-like, hanging outside the flower (8 marks)

In completing the statements for this answer you are bringing together information that would enable you to make a comparison of the two types of flowers. If you have time it would be a useful exercise to convert this information into continuous prose. Remember to use comparatives. For example, 'In insect-pollinated flowers the petals are larger and more colourful than those … etc'.

3 Insect visits flower to collect pollen/nectar
attracted by colour of petals/nectar
pollen collects on the insect's body
insect visits another flower
pollen transferred to the stigma of the flower
(if of the same type of flower) the pollen grains germinate/produce a pollen tube
pollen tube grows down the style to the ovule
male gametes move down the tube
to fertilise the egg cell nucleus
the ovule forms a seed
the wall of the ovary becomes modified to form a fruit (9 marks)

This question requires a lot of information for nine marks but it is straightforward and depends on accurate recall of facts. You should note that in the question the word insect is in bold print, as are the hints pollination, fertilisation, seed and fruit development. These are included to help you to organise your answer.

Unit 7

The Check Up

1 Can replicate/copy itself **2** Genes **3** Protein **4** Protein **5** Control rates of chemical reactions **6** Introduce foreign DNA into an organism **7** Genes with changed DNA **8** Randomly when DNA is copied **9** Identical **10** Half the chromosome number, i.e. '*n*' not '2*n*' **11** Double, i.e. '2*n*' not '*n*' **12** To reduce (halve) the number of chromosomes in the gametes **13** During meiosis Random fusion of gametes **14** Height **15** i) XY; ii) XX **16** One form of a gene **17** Zygote with two alleles that are the same **18** Gametes from left to right: male T and t, female T and t, offspring clockwise from top: Tt, tt, Tt, and TT **19** Red/green colour blindness or haemophilia **20** Environmental conditions determine which varieties survive and breed successfully and which varieties are less successful, possibly becoming extinct

Exam Practice

1 A double helix of DNA forms part of a **chromosome**. A small section of DNA constitutes a **gene**. The DNA of the gene codes for a specific **protein**. The protein may be a specific **enzyme** that controls a particular reaction in the **metabolism** of the cell. (4 marks)

One mark is scored for each of the points in bold type up to the maximum for the question.
If you have time in your revision programme you might like to try presenting the information for this answer in the form of an annotated diagram or flow chart.

2 a A gene is a short section of DNA
whereas an allele is one form of a gene (2 marks)
b A dominant gene is always expressed whatever allele it is paired with
but a recessive gene is only expressed when it is paired with another allele of the same type (2 marks)
c A gamete is haploid
whereas a zygote is diploid (2 marks)
d A homozygous individual has two of the same alleles for a particular gene
in contrast to a heterozygous individual that has two different alleles for the same gene (2 marks)

Note the use of the terms 'whereas', 'but' and 'in contrast' used to bring out the distinction asked for by the question.

3 *You may not have done any work specifically on the inheritance shown by guinea pigs but you will have met the principles necessary to answer this type of question. Do not be put off by questions based on 'novel' material.*

a i) BB ii) Bb (2 marks)
b i) Bb × Bb ii) Bb × bb (2 marks)
c bb
all gametes from the brown parent will carry b
homozygous blacks only produce one type of gamete, the dominant B
therefore all offspring from such a cross will be black
whereas heterozygous blacks produce two types of gametes, B and b
therefore offspring will be in ratio 1 black: 1 brown (4 marks)

This type of cross is called a 'test cross'.
It is important to use words such as 'therefore' or 'because' here because the question demands an explanation.

4 a carrier (1 mark)
b male gametes: X_H and Y
female gametes: X_H and X_h
genotypes of offspring: X_HX_H X_HX_h X_HY X_hY
phenotypes of offspring: normal female carrier female normal male haemophiliac male (4 marks)

You could write out checkerboards to investigate the outcome of other crosses if you have time.

Unit 8

The Check Up

1 Green plants **2** Primary consumer **3** Food web shows how each organism may be used by more than one consumer **4** Lions are predators. Zebra are prey animals OR Zebras are primary consumers/herbivores and lions are secondary consumers/carnivores **5** One from: spines/hairs/poisonous or unpalatable chemicals/leaves arranged as rosettes close to the ground **6** Drawing showing pyramidal shape with horizontal layers (as on p.41) **7** Dry mass of the organic matter of an organism **8** One from: respiration of organic material/loss by excretion/discarding of indigestible matter **9** Lost as heat to the environment **10** Fixes free carbon from carbon dioxide into organic compounds **11** Respiration and burning **12** Convert ammonium compounds into nitrates **13** Legumes **14** Reduces loss to pests during growth and storage **15** Pesticides can get into food chains and kill the 'wrong' organisms OR remain as residues in food **16** It is farmed or used for silviculture (cultivation of trees) **17** Three from: coal, peat, gas and oil **18** Carbon dioxide, sulphur dioxide and nitrogen oxides **19** Sulphur dioxide and nitrogen oxides **20** Loss of biodiversity/loss of carbon dioxide removers

Exam Practice

1 a Each or all of the species involved in a food web may be eaten by more than one consumer (1 mark)
b **C** (1 mark)
c plant material (1 mark)
d **C** → **B** → **D** → **A** (3 marks)

The marks are likely to be awarded according to the following scheme:
***C** before **B**; **B** before **D**; **D** before **A**; one mark each*

Do not be put off by information that you do not recognise. It is important that you should be able to extract relevant information from data. The question has been made more demanding by the inclusion of specific names. This forces you to consider all of the information, which might not have been necessary if the common names had been given.

2 a pyramid of numbers (1 mark)
b the main difference is at producer level
graph **B** has a smaller number of producers than primary consumers
therefore individually they must be larger plants/one tree (2 marks)
c i) total dry mass of the organic content of the organism(s) (1 mark)
ii) drawing of standard pyramid (see p. 41) for each (2 marks)

The stem asks for 'outlines' only, therefore you do not have to include the various trophic levels to gain the marks.

3 a i) green plants (2 marks)
ii) glucose (1 mark)
b i) aerobic respiration (1 mark)
ii) three from: respiration
decomposers
bacteria
fungi (3 marks)

4 a combustion of fossil fuels produces 'greenhouse gases'
carbon dioxide, sulphur dioxide and nitrogen oxides are greenhouse gases
large proportion of solar radiation is normally reflected from the Earth's surface back into space
but an increase in the concentration of greenhouse gases reduces this loss
therefore, because the combustion of fossil fuels has increased, so has the amount of heat trapped compared with the past (3 marks)

It is important to use words such as 'therefore' or 'because' in answers to questions demanding explanation.

b global warming
increase in the rate at which the polar ice caps melt
increase in sea levels
flooding of land currently above sea level
climatic changes
distribution of plant communities and dependent animal communities may change (3 marks)

Each point is worth a mark. You would not have to produce all of them to score maximum for the section. Take guidance as to how much to write from the number of marks available and the space the examiner suggests that you will need for your answer.

Unit 9

The Check Up

1 Dalton **2** The smallest part of an element that can exist alone **3** 1 amu, 0 **4** Negligible (or 0), –1 **5** Proton and electron **6** Contains only a proton or contains no neutrons **7** True **8 A** proton **B** electron **C** neutron **9** Nucleus **10** 15 **11** 15 **12** 16 **13** 15 **14** Protons + neutrons = 23 **15** 11 **16** 2,8,1 **17** Atoms of the same element containing different numbers of neutrons/Atoms of the same element having a different mass number but same atomic number **18** 35.5 **19** False **20** Electron

Exam Practice

1

Protons and neutrons in nucleus = 1 mark
Correct no. of p and n = 2 marks
Correct no. of e = 1 mark
Correct electron arrangement = 2 marks (6 marks)

2 a All three isotopes have 1 proton and 1 electron (1 mark)
Hydrogen-1 has no neutrons, hydrogen-2 has 1 neutron and hydrogen-3 has 2 neutrons (1mark)
b These three isotopes have identical chemical properties. (1 mark)
They have different physical properties (1 mark)

It is important that you include numbers and do not write that all three isotopes have the same number of protons and electrons but different numbers of neutrons.

3 a Both have 63 protons (1 mark)
Both have 63 electrons (1 mark)
Europium-151 has 88 neutrons (i.e. 151–63). Europium-153 has 90 neutrons (i.e. 153–63). (2 marks)

You must actually use the information to work out numbers of protons, neutrons and electrons.

b 152 (1 mark)

There are equal numbers of the two isotopes so the relative atomic mass is exactly halfway between. In many cases ,where figures do not work out easily you should expect to have to work out the answer with a calculator.

4 Atoms are the smallest particle of an element than can exist alone (1 mark)
but atoms are made up of protons, neutrons and electrons (1 mark)
protons and neutrons are packed together in the nucleus (1 mark)
electrons move around the nucleus in shells (1 mark)

5 a 16 protons, 16 neutrons and 16 electrons (3 marks)

The mass number is 32 and there are 16 electrons shown on the diagram. The number of protons is the same as the number of electrons. The number of neutrons is 32 – 16.

b 2,8,6 (1 mark)
c 2,6 (1 mark)
d Oxygen and sulphur atoms have six electrons in the outer shell/energy level (1 mark)

Oxygen is in the same group of the Periodic Table as sulphur and so has the same number of electrons in the outer shell/energy level.

Unit 10

The Check Up

1 Melting and boiling/evaporation **2** Gas **3** Liquid **4** Diffusion **5** Ionic **6** An electron from the sodium atom is lost and a chlorine atom gains an electron **7** Strong electrostatic forces between ions **8** Lattice **9** Covalent **10** Each atom gives one electron to be shared **11** Very weak forces between molecules **12** Covalent

13  ; **14** Ions Atoms **15** Loses two electrons

16 Gains two electrons **17** Mg^{2+} and O^{2-} **18** Strong forces involving ions with double charges **19** One magnesium ion is not associated with one chloride ion but they are present in equal numbers in a lattice **20** Diamond and graphite

Exam Practice

1 a 84 °C (1 mark)
b 80 °C (1 mark)

The answers for parts a and b come from the graph you have been given.

c **AB** Particles are moving freely (1 mark)
Slow down as temperature falls (1 mark)
BC Forces formed between particles as liquid solidifies (1 mark)
CD Particles only vibrate about fixed positions (1 mark)

It is important to describe what is happening in each portion of the graph and to comment on the forces involved and the movement of the particles.

d Energy released when forces formed maintains temperature (1 mark)

Remember that energy is required to break bonds so energy will be released when they are formed.

2 a About one third of the way along the tube from the hydrogen chloride end (1 mark)

This answer comes from the diagram.

b The ammonia particles move twice as fast as the hydrogen chloride particles (2 marks)
Or Ammonia particles move faster than hydrogen chloride particles (1 mark)

The quality of your answer to part b determines whether you score one or two marks.

c The particles are not travelling in a straight line (1 mark)
The tube is filled with air and particles of ammonia and hydrogen chloride collide with 'air' particles (1 mark)

3 a Diamond is a three-dimensional structure and all of the bonds are strong covalent bonds (1 mark)
b Bonds between carbon atoms in each layer are strong (1 mark) but the forces between the layers are weak (1 mark). This enables the layers to slide over each other (1 mark)

The common mistake here is to write that the forces in diamond are strong and the forces in graphite are weak.

4 a Molecules break up to form ions (1 mark)
Ions formed are H^+ and Cl^- (1 mark)

The clue to the change in bonding is the fact that the solution conducts electricity.

b Ionic bonding (1 mark)
Ions are Na^+ and H^- (1 mark)

It is unusual for hydrogen to form H^- ions. In a hydride ion the hydrogen atom gains an electron. The electron arrangement in a hydride ion is 2.

5 a Magnesium 2,8,2 (1 mark)
Oxygen 2,6 (1 mark)

This is using information from Revision Unit 9.

b Magnesium atom loses two electrons to form Mg^{2+} ion (1 mark)
Oxygen atom gains two electrons to form O^{2-} ion (1 mark)

A common mistake here is to refer to atoms swapping electrons. There is a complete transfer of electrons from a magnesium atom to an oxygen atom.

c The forces between ions in magnesium oxide are stronger because they are between ions with 2+ and 2– charges (1 mark)

Unit 11

The Check Up

1 M **2** NH_3 **3** Al_2O_3 **4** $2H_2 + O_2 \rightarrow 2H_2O$ **5** 100 **6** 80 g **7** (s) (l) (g) **8** 24 dm^3 **9** NO **10** N_2O **11** $4NH_3 + 5O_2 \rightarrow 4NO + 6H_2O$ **12** Reversible reaction **13** 6.9 g **14** 1.2 dm^3 **15** $2KHCO_3 + H_2SO_4 \rightarrow K_2SO_4 + 2H_2O + 2CO_2$ **16** 112 g **17** –184 kJ **18** Exothermic – negative value **19** 112 g **20** 2

Exam Practice

1 Two of the equations are correct. The corrected equations are:
a $2Al(s) + 6HCl(aq) \rightarrow 2AlCl_3(aq) + 3H_2(g)$
b $O^{2-}(s) + 2H^+(aq) \rightarrow H_2O(l)$
e $2K(s) + 2H_2O(l) \rightarrow 2KOH(aq) + H_2(g)$
f $CaCO_3(s) + H_2O(l) + CO_2(g) \rightarrow Ca(HCO_2)_3(aq)$ (4 marks)

Award 1 mark for each correct equation written. Deduct 1 mark if a correct equation has been altered. Higher level candidates should be able to write balanced symbol equations. It is important to use the correct formulae but also to check that the equation is balanced. The second equation is an ionic equation. There are two hydrogen particles and one oxygen particle on each side and the sum of the charges on each side is zero. This equation is true for all solid oxides reacting with any acid.

2 a KCl b ZnO c $ZnCO_3$ d $Zn(OH)_2$ e $Al(OH)_3$ f $AlPO_4$ g NH_4Cl h $(NH_4)_2SO_4$ i NH_4HCO_3 j $Fe_2(SO_4)_3$ (5 marks)

Each correct answer scores $\frac{1}{2}$ mark but round up the total to the nearest whole number. If you have time, use this table of ions to practise writing other formulae. One of the most distinguishing features of a Higher level candidate is the fluency at writing correct chemical formulae.

3 Mass of magnesium = 0.12 g
Mass of oxygen = 0.08 g (1 mark)
Number of mol of magnesium = 0.12/24 = 0.005 (1 mark)
Number of mol of oxygen = 0.08/16 = 0.005 (1 mark)
Equal numbers of magnesium and oxygen atoms (1 mark) so simplest formula is MgO

In this question you are given the answer. The marks are given for showing and explaining the steps you use to get the answer. The mass of magnesium is found by subtracting the first weighing from the second. The mass of oxygen is found by subtracting the second weighing from the third. The number of mol of magnesium is found by dividing the mass by the appropriate relative atomic mass. Too often a candidate writes the answer but does not convince the examiner that they know how to get this answer.

4 4.14 g of lead combines with 0.64 g of oxygen (1 mark)
4.14/207 mol of lead combines with 0.64/16 mol of oxygen (1 mark)
0.02 mol of lead combines with 0.04 mol of oxygen (1 mark)
The simplest formula is PbO_2 (1 mark)

The common mistake here is to score the first three marks but then to write the formula as Pb_2O. Remember that there are twice as many oxygen atoms as lead atoms.

5 a From the equation:
[40 + 12 + (3 × 16)] g of calcium carbonate forms [40 + (2 × 35.5)] g of calcium chloride (1 mark)
100 g of calcium carbonate forms 111 g of calcium chloride (1 mark)
10 g of calcium carbonate forms 11.1 g of calcium chloride (1 mark)

b 100 g of calcium carbonate forms 24 dm^3 of carbon dioxide at rtp (1 mark)
10 g of calcium carbonate forms 2.4 dm^3 of carbon dioxide (1 mark)

6 Energy required to break 1N≡N bond and 3H–H bonds = 944 + (3 × 436) = 2252 kJ (1 mark)
Energy released when 6 N–H bonds formed = (6 × 388) = 2328 kJ (1 mark)
Energy change = 2252–2328 = –76 kJ (1 mark)

The negative value shows that the reaction is exothermic.

Unit 12

The Check Up

1 Period **2** Group **3** Mendeleev **4** Noble gases **5** Atomic mass **6** Atomic number **7** Alkali metals **8** Lithium **9** Halogens **10** Fluorine **11** Transition metals **12** Metals, non-metals (both required in correct order) **13** Right-hand side towards top **14** Aluminium **15** Helium **16** Hydrogen **17** Lithium **18** Germanium **19** Increases **20** Decreases

Exam Practice

1 a Both melting points and boiling points decrease down the group (2 marks)

You are looking for patterns here from the data. There is one mark for seeing the pattern in melting points and one in boiling points.

b Melting point: in the range 30–45 °C (1 mark)
Boiling point: in the range 650–730 °C (1 mark)

It is impossible to be exact here and the word predict indicates this. Look at the gap in melting point between lithium and sodium and between sodium and potassium. It is decreasing. Assuming it decreases again you should predict within the range given.

c Any three of the following:
potassium floats on water, it fizzes, it disappears, reacts rapidly, pinkish lilac flame, it spits (3 marks)

The marks here are given for observations not for the chemistry of the reaction. The question is testing whether you have seen the reaction.

d As the group is descended the atoms get larger (1 mark)
The outer electron is more easily lost (1 mark)
because it is further from the nucleus (1 mark)

You could improve the quality of your answer by including the equation:
$M \rightarrow M^+ + e^-$ *where M represents any alkali metal atom*

2 a i) Colourless to brown (2 marks)

Many candidates forget that the question is about colour change so the colour must be given before and after.

ii) $2KI + Cl_2 \rightarrow 2KCl + I_2$ (2 marks)

One mark is for the correct formulae and one is for balancing. This question highlights the importance of being able to write balanced symbol equations for success on Higher tier papers.

b i) Hydrogen chloride (1 mark)
ii) $H_2 + Cl_2 \rightarrow 2HCl$ (2 marks)

One mark for correct formulae and one for balancing. The frequent mistake is to forget that molecules of both hydrogen and chlorine are made up of pairs of atoms.

c i) Fluorine (1 mark)
It is the most reactive halogen (1 mark)

Too often candidates think the reactivity increases down the group (like group 1). They often misspell fluorine as flourine.

ii) It was believed that noble gases such as xenon were completely unreactive. This reaction proved that they are not (1 mark)

3 a Argon and potassium *or* tellurium and iodine *or* cobalt and nickel (1 mark)

b In the modern Periodic Table elements are arranged in order of increasing atomic number (1 mark)
Argon, atomic number 18, is before potassium, atomic number 19
or tellurium, atomic number 52, is before iodine, atomic number 53
or cobalt, atomic number 27, is before nickel, atomic number 28 (1 mark)

c Each step across the Periodic Table increases the number of protons by one (1 mark)
However there is no pattern to the increase in the number of neutrons (1 mark)

Unit 13

The Check Up

1 Compounds of carbon and hydrogen **only** **2** Compounds containing only single bonds **3** C_2H_6 and C_8H_{18} **4** Methane CH_4 **5** Crude oil or petroleum **6** Fractional distillation **7** Petrol **8** C_3H_8 **9** Carbon dioxide and water **10** Carbon monoxide and water **11** Cracking **12** Making polymers (plastics) **13** Ethene C_2H_4 **14** A carbon-carbon double bond **15** Red or brown to colourless (not clear) **16** 1,2-dibromoethane **17** Isomers **18** Compound of carbon, hydrogen and oxygen fitting a formula $C_x(H_2O)_y$ **19** Ethanol and carbon dioxide **20** Fermentation

Exam Practice

1 a Test each compound with a solution of bromine (1 mark)
No change with chloroethane (1 mark)
Solution turns colourless with chloroethene (1 mark)

This is a test for a carbon-carbon double bond. It is important to give the reagent and what happens with each carbon compound. With chloroethene writing 'red or brown to colourless' is acceptable but 'discolours' or 'turns clear' are not.

b i) Hydrogen chloride, HCl (1 mark)
ii) Addition (1 mark)

c i) Polymerisation (1 mark)
ii)

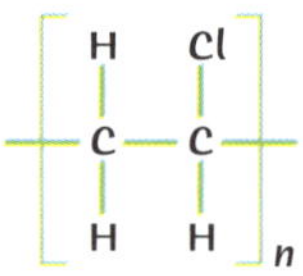

One mark for showing a chain and one mark for the double bond being changed to a single bond.

(2 marks)

d Does not soften on wetting, stronger (2 marks)

There are other possible answers, e.g. polymers can be easily moulded. However, cost is not acceptable.

2 a C_5H_{12} (1 mark)

b

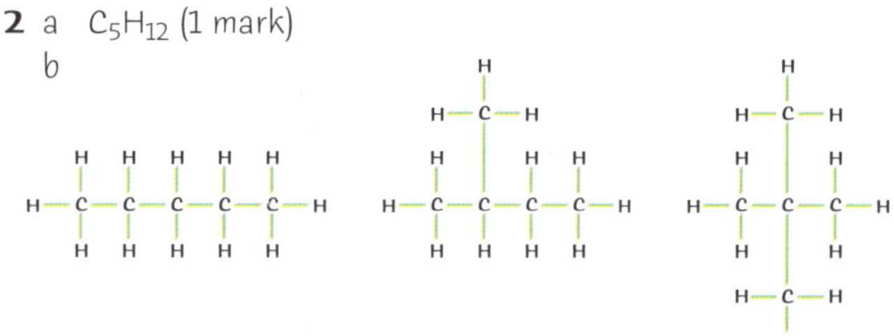

(3 marks)

3 a Mixtures of methane and air are explosive (1 mark)

b In excess air, carbon dioxide and water are produced (1 mark)
$CH_4 + 2O_2 \rightarrow CO_2 + 2H_2O$ (1 mark)
In limited air, carbon monoxide and water are produced (1 mark)
$2CH_4 + 3O_2 \rightarrow 2CO + 4H_2O$ (1 mark)

This question is very testing and requires a lot of information for four marks. The most frequent mistake is to give hydrogen as one of the products.

4 Crude oil was formed millions of years ago by the action of **high temperatures** and **high pressures** on the remains of **living sea creatures** in the **absence of air or oxygen**. (4 marks)
The crude oil is trapped between **impermeable rocks** in traps formed by **folding rocks** (2 marks)

One mark is scored for each of the points in bold type. A labelled diagram could be an alternative for the second part (see The Crash Course on p. 60).

Unit 14

The Check Up

1 Reactivity series(or activity series) **2** Bauxite **3** Electrolysis **4** Alumina has a very high melting point/reduces melting point of electrolyte **5** $Al^{3+} + 3e^- \rightarrow Al$, $2O^{2-} \rightarrow O_2 + 4e^-$ **6** Haematite **7** Coke and limestone **8** Carbon monoxide **9** Slag **10** Steel **11** Aluminium oxide is more difficult to split up (or aluminium is higher in the reactivity series) **12** Hydrogen **13** Zinc or iron **14** Copper/silver/gold/platinum **15** Zinc sulphate and copper **16** Displacement reaction **17** Alloy **18** Magnesium, magnesium oxide, magnesium hydroxide, magnesium carbonate **19** Precipitation **20** $H^+ + OH^- \rightarrow H_2O$

Exam Practice

1 a $CuO + H_2SO_4 \rightarrow CuSO_4 + H_2O$ (2 marks)

b Warm sulphuric acid;
add copper(II) oxide; continue until copper(II) oxide remains unreacted;
filter off excess copper(II) oxide;
evaporate solution;
until only a small volume of solution remains;
leave to cool and crystallise (6 marks)

There are eight marking points here. One mark should be awarded for each point made up to a maximum of six. Common errors are:
- *not adding copper(II) oxide until in excess*
- *writing that the copper(II) oxide does not continue to dissolve as the solution is saturated. The copper(II) oxide reacts and uses up dilute sulphuric acid so when the copper(II) oxide remains it is because all the acid has been used up.*
- *evaporating the solution to dryness will decompose the copper(II) sulphate crystals.*

2 a Displacement or exothermic or redox reaction (1 mark)

b $Fe_2O_3 + 2Al \rightarrow Al_2O_3 + 2Fe$ (2 marks)

One mark for writing correct formulae and one mark for balancing.

c Magnesium (1 mark)

Magnesium is in a similar position to aluminium in the reactivity series. Sodium is too reactive.

3 a Ore; reduction; coke; carbon monoxide; calcium oxide; slag; steel (6 marks)

There are seven spaces. Seven correct answers score 6 marks,six scores 5 marks, five scores 4 marks. This continues until two correct scores 1 mark.

The mistake candidates make here is not to read the whole passage after filling the spaces. If this is done obvious mistakes are seen and can be corrected.

b Limestone decomposes into calcium oxide and carbon dioxide (1 mark)
$CaCO_3 \rightarrow CaO + CO_2$ (1 mark)
Calcium oxide (basic oxide) reacts with silicon(IV) oxide (acidic oxide) (1 mark)
$CaO + SiO_2 \rightarrow CaSiO_3$ (1 mark)

c i) Carbon dioxide is turned into carbon monoxide which is the active reducing agent (1 mark)
ii) Reaction of carbon with oxygen (1 mark)
Decomposition of calcium carbonate (1 mark)
or Reaction of carbon monoxide with iron(III) oxide (1 mark)

Unit 15

The Check Up

1 Rate decreases **2** Substance which alters the rate of a reaction without being used up **3** As catalysts are not used up they can continue to act **4** Enzyme **5** Coal dust has a much larger surface area **6** Magnesium and hydrochloric acid (2 mol/dm^3) – more concentrated **7** Sunlight provides energy to start the reaction (it breaks some chlorine molecules into chlorine atoms) **8** Lower temperatures slow down reactions causing food to go bad **9** Higher temperature (and higher humidity) speeds up reaction **10** Raising temperature causes particles to move faster, producing more frequent and effective collisions **11** Dynamic equilibrium **12** Haber process **13** $N_2 + 3H_2 \rightleftharpoons 2NH_3$ **14** Fractional distillation of liquid air **15** Reacting methane/natural gas or naphtha with steam **16** Iron (or iron(III) oxide) **17** Recycled **18** By liquefying **19** Low temperature and high pressure **20** Ammonium sulphate $(NH_4)_2SO_4$

Exam Practice

1 a **D** (1 mark)
Half the mass of $CaCO_3$ produces half the volume of CO_2 (1 mark)
D is the only graph producing half the volume of CO_2 (1 mark)

b **B** (1 mark)
Crushing the marble chips gives a much larger surface area of calcium carbonate (1 mark)
so graph is steeper (1 mark)

c Sue should measure the loss of mass (1 mark)
caused by the escaping carbon dioxide gas (1 mark)
at regular intervals (1 mark)

This method cannot be used for reactions involving hydrogen, e.g. magnesium and hydrochloric acid, because of the very low density of hydrogen. It is important to mention time as rate cannot be calculated without it. In practice the reactants are put into a flask standing on a top-pan balance. A piece of cotton wool is placed in the neck of the flask, not to stop gas escaping but to ensure no acid spray escapes.

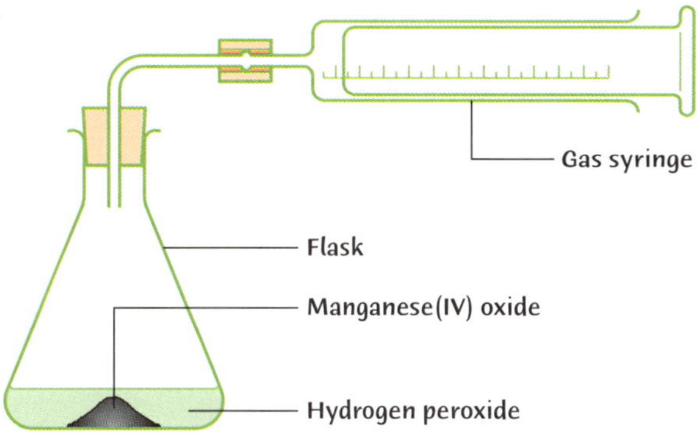

2 a *One mark for suitable reacting vessel, e.g. flask, one mark for piece of measuring apparatus, e.g. gas syringe, measuring cylinder or burette.*
Deduct 1 mark if apparatus not air-tight.
1 mark for apparatus correctly labelled.

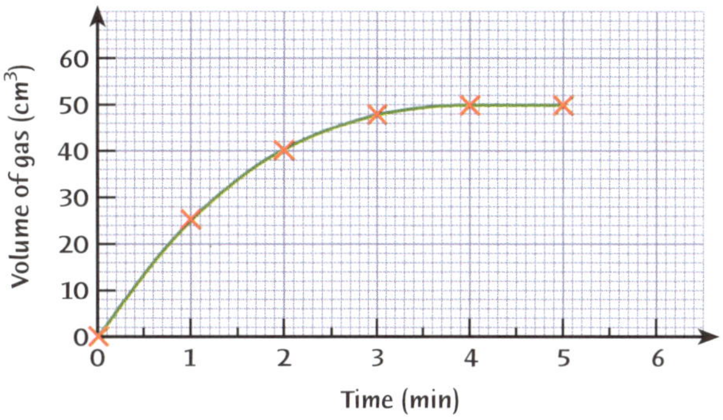

b *Volume on y-axis, time on x-axis* (1 mark)
Axes labelled and good scales (1 mark)
Points correctly plotted (1 mark)
Curve through points (1 mark)

This is a good example of a graph on a Higher tier paper where decisions have to be made about scales and axes. In addition there could be anomalous points.

c i) *Your sketched graph should be less steep than the one you plotted* (1 mark) *but reach the same maximum of 50 cm^3* (1 mark)
ii) The particles are more widely spaced (1 mark) so there are fewer (effective) collisions (1 mark)

d 25 cm^3 of H_2O_2 produces 50 cm^3 of oxygen so hydrogen peroxide is 2 volume (1 mark)

Candidates find this type of calculation difficult but all the information needed is in the question.

e The substances that work all contain metals which form at least two different positive ions (1 mark). The ones that do not work contain a metal which only forms one positive ion (1 mark)

The frequent mistake here is to state that the ones that work contain transition metals. This is not correct because lead is not a transition metal.

f i) Enzyme or biological catalyst (1 mark)
ii) At higher temperature the enzyme is denatured, i.e. the protein structure is irreversibly damaged (1 mark)

A frequent answer here is 'the enzymes are killed'. This is not a creditworthy answer. All of this topic is included in Single Award except enzymes which are Double Award only.

Unit 16

The Check Up

1 A core **B** mantle **C** crust **2** Igneous **3** Marble **4** Conglomerate or limestone **5** Intrusive - crystallised within the Earth; extrusive - crystallised on the Earth's surface **6** Large crystals indicate slow cooling; small crystals indicate fast cooling **7** High temperatures and high pressures **8** Any four from: erosion, weathering, transportation, deposition, compaction, cementation **9** Igneous **10** Alfred Wegener **11** Solar and nuclear energy **12** Earthquakes occur when two plates rub together **13** Europe and USA are on different plates and the plates are moving apart or there is a constructive plate boundary between the two plates **14** Two continental plates colliding with one another and one is pushed upwards **15** Combustion, respiration and corrosion **16** Photosynthesis **17** Reduction in carbon dioxide and increase in oxygen **18** Burning of increased amounts of fossil fuels or destruction of forests **19** Oceanic plate/the denser plate **20** Melts back into the mantle

Exam Practice

1 **1** melting **2** crystallising **3** erosion **4** compacting **5** high temperature and high pressure **6** erosion **7** erosion
One mark for each correct answer (7 marks)

2 Earthquakes usually occur at plate boundaries (1 mark)
There are some earthquakes which do not occur at plate boundaries (1 mark)

At this point compare the distribution of earthquakes with the plate boundaries (see the diagram on page 73).

3 South America and Africa were once joined (1 mark)
They are on different plates and these plates are moving apart (1 mark)

You could trace the outlines of South America and Africa and see how well they fit together.

4 The oceanic plate moves under the continental plate (1 mark)
Because the oceanic plate is denser (1 mark)
the oceanic plate melts into the magma or the continental plate is pushed upwards (1 mark)
see the diagram (at the top of the next column) (1 mark)

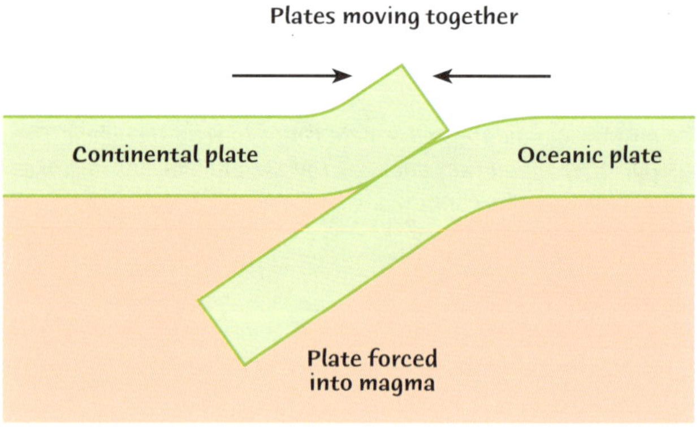

The Andes mountains in South America were formed by a continental plate and an oceanic plate moving together.

5 $4FeCO_3(s) + O_2(g) \rightarrow 2Fe_2O_3(s) + 4CO_2(g)$ (4 marks)

This equation is difficult but is worth four marks. One mark is for the correct formulae of iron(II) carbonate and iron(III) oxide, one mark for the correct formulae of oxygen and carbon dioxide, one mark for balancing and one mark for correct state symbols. Iron(II) is being oxidised to iron(III).

Reaction produces carbon dioxide and uses up oxygen (1 mark)
The equation shows 1 mol of oxygen produces 4 mol of carbon dioxide. (1 mark)

This is an example of using information from an equation without having to carry out a calculation.

6 a **B** (1 mark)

In the diagram the oldest rocks are at the bottom and the newest rocks are nearest to the surface.

b **D** (1 mark)
c **C** (1 mark)
d **D** (1 mark)

Unit 17

The Check Up

1 A series circuit has only one path for the current; a parallel circuit has more than one path **2** The ammeter is represented by an A in the circle drawn to the left of the cell. The voltmeter is represented by a V in the circle drawn in parallel with the lamp **3** A variable resistor. It is used to change the current in a circuit **4** energy battery lamp **5** So that each lamp can be switched individually **6** The ohm, Ω **7** Diode **8** Thermistor **9** Light-dependent resistor (LDR) **10 A** neutral **B** earth **C** live **D** fuse **11** To cut off the current if it becomes too great **12** Live **13** Earth **14** Earth wire and fuse **15** Alternating current changes direction **16** 17.0 V **17** 12 Ω **18** It increases **19** 2040 W **20** £1.96

Exam Practice

1 **A1** 1.2 A (1 mark)
A2 1.2 A (1 mark)
A3 1.7 A (1 mark)
V1 6.5 V (1 mark)
V2 6.5 V (1 mark)

The total current passing out of a junction in a parallel circuit is equal to the current that enters the junction.
Components connected in parallel always have the same voltage across them.

2 a power = current × voltage (1 mark)
= 3.8 A × 240 V (1 mark)
= 912 W (1 mark)

Always write down the formula first. Then, even if you make a mistake in the calculation, you gain one mark for knowledge of the correct formula. Finally, do not forget to include the correct unit with your answer. A wrong unit or no unit at all loses the third mark.

b 5 A (1 mark)
This allows the normal current to pass, but should break the circuit if the current becomes too great (1 mark)

When choosing a fuse, choose the rating immediately above the normal current.

c resistance = voltage ÷ current (1 mark)
= 240 V ÷ 3.8 A (1 mark)
= 63.2 Ω (1 mark)

d The element is cold (1 mark)
so the resistance is less (1 mark)

You are not expected to know about the change in resistance of a toaster. In this question you are being asked to apply your knowledge about the change in resistance of a lamp filament to a similar situation.

e i) The metal case (1 mark)
ii) The case could become live, giving a danger of electrocution (1 mark)

Touching a live object creates a complete circuit through the person to earth.

iii) A large current passes to earth (1 mark)
The fuse melts and breaks the circuit (1 mark)

Avoid using terms such as 'the fuse blows'. Always try to be as precise and technically correct as possible in your answers.

f i) There is no earth wire (1 mark)
The plastic case does not conduct electricity (1 mark)
So it cannot become live (1 mark)
ii) 0.160 kW × 8 hours (1 mark)
= 1.28 kWh (1 mark)

The first mark in this question is for a correct conversion from W to kW.

iii) 1.28 × 7p = 8.96p (1 mark)

If your answer to part ii) was wrong, you can still gain the mark here by using the wrong answer correctly.

Unit 18

The Check Up

1 Similar charges repel, opposite charges attract **2** Electrons move from the duster to the polythene. **3** Charge passes easily through the copper **4** It can cause a spark **5** It removes dust from the exhaust gases **6** electrons negative positive **7** Both positive and negative ions move in the gas **8** 135 C **9** Similar poles repel, opposite poles attract **10** The direction of the force on a north-seeking pole **11** Reverse the current. Reverse the magnetic field direction **12** The force on the left-hand side should be down and that on the right-hand side should be up. **13** By moving the coil or the magnet **14** Two from: speed of movement, strength of magnet, number of turns on coil **15** Reverse the direction of movement. Reverse the magnetic poles **16** It increases the size of an alternating voltage **17** A step-up transformer has more turns on the secondary than on the primary. The reverse is true for a step-down transformer **18** 16 000 **19** To minimise energy losses **20** By using step-down transformers

Exam Practice

1 a The bag gains electrons (1 mark)
The cloth loses electrons (1 mark)

Electrostatic charging occurs whenever two surfaces rub together. The material that gains electrons becomes negatively charged, and the material that loses electrons becomes positively charged.

b i) Charge passes through the copper strip (1 mark) then through the person to earth (1 mark)

People are good conductors of small amounts of charge. If your body becomes charged by walking across a nylon carpet, you feel a slight shock when you touch an earthed object. The shock is due to the current in your body as the charge passes to earth.

ii) Yes, there is still electron transfer between the cloth and the copper strip (1 mark)
iii) Isolate it from the earth by using a good electrical insulator (1 mark)

In a van de Graaff generator, charge builds up on a metal dome. The dome has to be well insulated from the earth.

2 a i) current = charge flow ÷ time (1 mark)
= 9.0 C ÷ 60 s (1 mark)
= 0.15 A (1 mark)

The first mark is for knowledge of the formula. Always write this down in the form that you have learned it before attempting to rearrange it.

To gain the third mark, you need to have the correct unit as well as the correct numerical answer.

ii) Electrons (1 mark)
From negative to positive (1 mark)

b Positive ions move from positive to negative (1 mark)
Negative ions move from negative to positive (1 mark)

3 a i) The magnetic field through the copper conductors is changing (1 mark)
This causes an induced voltage (1 mark)

Always emphasise the changing magnetic field when explaining electromagnetic induction effects.

ii) The size of the voltage changes (1 mark)
The frequency of the voltage changes (1 mark)

The mains voltage alternates at 50 Hz. One complete cycle is generated for each revolution of the electromagnet.

b i) Two coils of wire (1 mark)
Wound on an iron core (1 mark)
The secondary (output) coil has more turns than the primary (input) coil (1 mark)
ii) It decreases it (1 mark)

As the power output cannot be greater than the power input, an increase in voltage is accompanied by a decrease in current.

iii) The current causes heating in the transmission wires (1 mark)
The smaller the current, the less energy is wasted as heat (1 mark)
iv) Transformers could not be used to change the size of the voltage (1 mark)
As transformers rely on the changing magnetic field due to an alternating current (1 mark)

Transformers are efficient devices for changing the size of an alternating voltage. That is why the mains uses a.c. There is no equivalent device for changing the size of a direct voltage.

Unit 19

The Check Up

1 Equal to **2** pulls equal opposite **3** Earth pulling person **4 D 5 A 6 D 7 B** and **C 8** The forcemeter would not return to zero. The scale would be non-linear **9** The force acts over a small area, creating a large pressure **10** 1200 Pa **11** 3.79×10^5 N **12** There is no force from the inside to balance the large push of the air from outside **13** 0.05 m^2 **14** 1.0×10^5 Pa **15** In all directions **16** By the fluid pushing on a platform with a large area **17** By collisions between the gas particles and the container walls **18** The pressure decreases because the collisions are less frequent **19** It becomes five times as great **20** $P_1V_1 = P_2V_2$

Exam Practice

1 a The downwards force is the pull (1 mark) of the Earth (1 mark) (2 marks)
The upwards force is the push (1 mark) of the spring (1 mark) (2 marks)

Avoid the term 'gravity' when describing forces as it is often used to mean several different things.

b The forces are equal in size (1 mark)
because the person is not moving (1 mark)

When an object is not moving, the forces acting on it must be balanced, i.e. is equal-sized forces act in opposite directions.

2 a Pressure = force ÷ area (1 mark)
= 150 N ÷ 7.5×10^{-4} m^2 (1 mark)
= 2.0×10^5 Pa (1 mark)

When small areas are involved, it is acceptable to work out the pressure in N/cm², in this case giving an answer of 20 N/cm².

b 2.0×10^5 Pa or 20 N/cm² (1 mark)

Solids transmit force, but fluids transmit pressure equally in all directions.

c Force = pressure × area (1 mark)
= 2.0×10^5 Pa × 30×10^{-4} m^2
= 600 N (1 mark)

The first mark is for rearranging the pressure formula correctly. The second mark is for the correct answer and unit.

d Hydraulic brakes magnify force (1 mark)
With hydraulic brakes, it is easy to transmit the pressure round corners (1 mark)

3 a The pressure is due to collisions (1 mark)
Between the particles and the container walls (1 mark)

A common misconception it this level is that the gas pressure is due to collisions between the particles.

b $P_1V_1 = P_2V_2$ (1 mark)
$V_2 = (P_1V_1)/P_2$ = 1.25×10^6 Pa × 120 cm³ ÷ 1.01×10^5 Pa (1 mark)
= 1485 cm³ (1 mark)

When using the pressure law, it is not necessary to change volumes into m³, so long as the units used on each side of the equation are consistent.

c When the gas stops leaving the cylinder, it is still full of 120 cm³ gas at atmospheric pressure (1 mark)

If you open the valve on a bicycle tyre, all the air does not come out of the tyre. Air flows through the valve until the pressures on each side are equal.

Unit 20

The Check Up

1 average speed = distance travelled ÷ time taken **2** 2.4 s **3** the speed **4** its direction **5** movement in the opposite direction to that which is positive **6** acceleration = increase in velocity ÷ time taken **7** m/s² **8** the slope or gradient **9** the distance travelled during a driver's reaction time **10** the distance travelled while the vehicle is braking **11** stopping distance = thinking distance + braking distance **12** 2500 N backwards **13 C 14 B 15 C 16 A 17 C 18** force = mass × acceleration **19** The weight (pull of the Earth) downwards. The resistive force (push of the air) upwards **20** 650 N

Exam Practice

1 a 16 s (1 mark)

The car travelled at a constant speed between the times 15 s and 31 s shown on the graph.

b **A**, **D** and **E** (1 mark for two correct) (2 marks)

*Note that on sections **D** and **E** the car was increasing its speed in the opposite direction to the initial direction of travel.*

c 28 m/s (1 mark)

Award the mark even if you answered –28 m/s, but note that speed only has size, unlike velocity it does not have a direction.

d The car accelerated (1 mark)
It changed direction (1 mark)

e Initial velocity = 6 m/s Final velocity = 24 m/s (1 mark)
acceleration = increase in velocity ÷ time taken (1 mark)
= (24 m/s – 6 m/s) ÷ 15 s (1 mark)
= 1.2 m/s^2 (1 mark)

You must have both the answer and the unit correct to gain the last mark. If your readings from the graph were wrong, you can still gain the final three marks provided that your calculation is correct for your readings.

An equivalent unit for acceleration is ms^{-2} but m/s/s is wrong as it is ambiguous.

f distance travelled = average speed × time (1 mark)
= 12 m/s × 4 s (1 mark)
= 48 m (1 mark)

A common error is to omit the 'average' from 'average speed'. This would give an answer of 96 m, and gain two marks out of three. Because the car was slowing down from a speed of 24 m/s to one of 0 m/s, it only travelled half this distance.

2 a acceleration = force ÷ mass (1 mark)
= 120 N ÷ 80 kg (1 mark)
= 1.5 m/s^2 (1 mark)

Again, you must have the correct answer and unit for the final mark.

b It increases (1 mark)

The resistive force increases as there is more air to be pushed out of the way each second when the cyclist speeds up.

c The unbalanced force decreases (1 mark)
So the acceleration decreases (1 mark)

Explain means 'give the reason'. Questions involving force, mass and acceleration are common on Higher tier papers.

d 120 N (1 mark)

When the cyclist is travelling at a constant speed on the level, the driving and resistive forces are balanced.

e i) Thinking distance = speed × time = 12 m/s × 0.6 s = 7.2 m (1 mark)
Braking distance = average speed x time = 6 m/s (1 mark) × 1.5 s = 9 m (2 marks)
Stopping distance = 7.2 m + 9 m = 16.2 m (1 mark)

Note that there is a mark here for realising that the average speed during braking is 6 m/s.

ii) It could increase as water reduces the friction between the wheels and the brakes (1 mark)

Unit 21

The Check Up

1 waves per second **2** hertz (Hz) **3** wave speed = frequency × wavelength **4** In a longitudinal wave, the vibrations are parallel to the direction of wave travel. In a transverse wave the vibrations are at right angles to the direction of wave travel **5** longitudinal **6** 'Sound' waves with a frequency above the range of human hearing **7** One from: For measuring distances or scanning body tissue **8 A** reflection **B** refraction **C** diffraction **9** refraction **10** The wavelength and the size of the gap **11** transverse **12** the greatest displacement from the mean position **13** less than the critical angle **14** total internal reflection **15** Light has a very short wavelength, so a very small gap is needed for spreading to occur **16** Microwaves and infra-red **17** Radio waves **18** They can pass through body tissue and damage cells **19** They pass through flesh but are absorbed by bone **20** Ultraviolet

Exam Practice

1 a wavelength = speed ÷ frequency (1 mark)
= 1500 m/s ÷ 50 000 Hz (1 mark)
= 0.03 m (1 mark)

The first mark is for knowledge of the formula in any correct form. To gain the third mark, you must have the correct unit as well as the numerical answer.

b distance travelled = speed × time (1 mark)
= 1500 m/s × 0.30 s = 450 m (1 mark)
As the pulse has travelled to the bottom of the lake and back, the depth of the lake is half this, i.e. 225 m (1 mark)

This is a common type of question at GCSE. There is also a very common error – forgetting to halve the total distance travelled to find the depth of the lake.

c The time is reduced (1 mark)
as the ultrasound has less distance to travel (1 mark)

2 a i) The angle of incidence (1 mark) must be greater than (1 mark) the critical angle (1 mark) (3 marks)

Note that there are marks awarded here for precise use of the correct scientific terminology. Many GCSE candidates lose marks by not doing this, and by using everyday ambiguous terms. Make sure that your meaning is absolutely clear.

ii) Any one from: cycle (or car) reflector, camera, periscope, binoculars (1 mark)

b i) The diagram should show light being reflected from the inner surface of the fibre (1 mark), the reflected light making the same angle with the surface as the incident light (1 mark) (2 marks)

Take care to be as precise with diagrams as you are with words. Sloppy drawing could easily cost a mark here.

ii) By using another fibre to carry the reflected light to the eye (1 mark)

iii) One from:
X-rays can damage cells
Optical fibres enable the workings of the body to be studied over time (1 mark)

The cue word 'suggest' means that you are not meant to have a detailed knowledge of the situation, but to be able to apply what you do know and understand about fibre optics.

3 a frequency = speed ÷ wavelength (1 mark)
= 3.00×10^8 m/s ÷ 3.00 m (1 mark)
= 1.00×10^8 Hz (1 mark)

A common error is to write down the answer as 1.00^{08}. This is incorrect and is a wrong interpretation of the calculator display.

b The gap is narrow compared to the wavelength of the long wave broadcast (1 mark)

so diffraction causes spreading as the waves pass through the gap (1 mark)
The gap is wide compared to the wavelength of the VHF broadcast (1 mark)
so very little spreading occurs as the waves pass through the gap (1 mark)

When answering questions about the diffraction of waves, always emphasise the size of the opening compared to the wavelength.

c Everyday openings such as doorways are very many wavelengths wide for light, so little spreading occurs (1 mark)
They are comparable to the wavelength of sound, which is diffracted round the edges (1 mark)

Unit 22

The Check Up

1 one **2** Mercury has the greatest orbital speed and the shortest distance to travel **3** transverse **4** the outer core is liquid, the inner core is solid **5** equal to **6** they are closer to the Sun, so the Sun's radiation is more intense **7** the asteroid belt **8** Pluto **9** Jupiter is more massive than the Earth **10** Any two from: surveillance, astronomy, navigation, communication, weather forecasting **11** evaporation of ice and gases from the head of the comet **12** at its closest point to the Sun **13** comet orbits are highly elliptical; comets can orbit in any direction **14** gravitational **15** it cools **16** Main sequence Red supergiant White dwarf **17** it all started at a single point **18** a very bright, exploding star **19** it explodes to form a neutron star and a cloud of dust **20** the 'big bang'

Exam Practice

1 a i) Jupiter (1 mark)

Jupiter has the highest surface gravitational field strength, which is the weight/kg of a mass placed at its surface.

ii) Pluto (1 mark)
b Jupiter (1 mark)

Jupiter takes the shortest time to rotate on its own axis.

c i) Pluto (1 mark)
ii) Pluto has the lowest orbital speed (1 mark) and it has the greatest orbital distance (1 mark)
d i) For a suitable choice of scale, with axes labelled with both the quantity and the unit (1 mark)
For correct plotting of the four points (2 marks)
(1 mark if one or two are incorrectly plotted)
For drawing a smooth curve (1 mark)

You will only be asked to choose scales and label axes on the parts of the examination paper that are exclusive to Higher tier. A grid with axes and scales will be given on questions that also appear on the Foundation tier papers.

ii) As the distance from the Sun increases, the mean orbital speed decreases (1 mark)
iii) The Sun's gravitational field strength decreases with increasing distance from the Sun (1 mark)

To understand how the Sun's pull affects the orbital speed, fasten a rubber bung to a length of string and whirl it in a horizontal circle. The harder you pull the string, the faster it goes.

iv) 6.8 km/s (1 mark) (allow 6.7 to 6.9 km/s)

The whole of this question is concerned with data analysis, an important scientific skill. Examiners often put data analysis questions in the context of astronomy because there is very little subject knowledge required in this section of the national curriculum.

2 a The force increases as Mercury approaches the Sun (1 mark)
And decreases as Mercury goes away from the Sun (1 mark)
The direction is always towards the Sun (1 mark)

Remember that forces have both size and direction, so you need to describe any changes in both of these.

b It is the same size (1 mark)
And in the opposite direction (1 mark)

Although each body exerts the same size force on the other, the Sun has the greater effect because Mercury has much less mass.

c The days are hot (1 mark)
The nights are cold (1 mark)

Mercury has no atmosphere, so there is no 'greenhouse effect' to reduce the cooling down at night.

3 a Gravitational forces caused part of the dust cloud to collapse (1 mark)
This caused heating (1 mark)
Eventually it became hot enough for a fusion reaction to begin (1 mark)

Contraction always causes heating, and expansion causes cooling. A star becomes a star when it starts to give out its own light.

b It will expand to a red giant (1 mark)
Then it will contract to a white dwarf (1 mark)

Unit 23

The Check Up

1 evaporation **2** convection **3** radiation **4** evaporation **5** dark/dull **6** dark/dull **7** The trapped air and plastic are poor conductors **8** The trapped air cannot move to form a convection current **9** It reduces (reflects) energy loss by radiation and it prevents evaporation **10** convection **11** More can be grown during the Earth's lifetime **12** Any two from: coal, oil, natural gas **13** 38% of the energy from the coal is transferred to electricity **14** To conserve fossil fuels **15** 2400 J **16** Energy from gravitational potential energy is transferred to kinetic energy (and some goes to heat) **17** By polishing the slide to reduce the friction force **18** 980 J **19** 360 J **20** 360 J

Exam Practice

1 a i) Energy is passed on from more energetic particles to less energetic ones (1 mark)

In a metal, free electrons aid the conduction process. This is why metals are much better conductors than non-metals.

ii) Air near the surface becomes warmed and expands (1 mark)
This air is less dense than the surrounding air and rises (1 mark)

Common misconceptions among GCSE candidates include 'heat rises' and 'heat particles rise'. Neither will gain credit in an examination. Always describe convection in terms of the movement of denser and less dense parts of the fluid.

iii) Energy is given off as infra-red (1 mark) electromagnetic radiation (1 mark) (2 marks)

Hot objects also radiate energy as light and other types of electromagnetic radiation.

b The cover stops convection currents (1 mark) and evaporation (1 mark) (2 marks)

Evaporation is the major way in which a warm liquid cools. This is why a simple plastic cover is so effective at reducing the energy loss from a swimming pool.

2 a Three suggestions from:
they conserve fossil fuels; they do not cause atmospheric pollution; the running costs are low; they provide a renewable energy source (1 mark each) (3 marks)

An answer such as 'they do not cause pollution' would not gain any marks. The type of pollution referred to needs to be specific. A reference to carbon dioxide or sulphur dioxide is an acceptable alternative to 'atmospheric'.

b Three suggestions from:
they are noisy; they are thought by some people to be unsightly; they take up large areas of land; installation costs are high (1 mark each) (3 marks)

The answers to a and b both refer to costs. You must distinguish between installation costs and running costs to gain the marks.

3 a work done = force × distance moved in its direction (1 mark)
= 600 N × 150 m (1 mark)
= 90 000 J (1 mark)

b power = work done ÷ time taken
= 90 000 J ÷ 20 s (1 mark)
= 4500 (1 mark)
W (1 mark)

A mark has not been given for knowing the formula here, as this is a formula that is provided on examination papers. Instead, there is a separate mark for knowledge of the correct unit. This can be awarded even if the final answer is wrong.

c kinetic energy = $\frac{1}{2}$ × mass × (velocity)^2
= $\frac{1}{2}$ × 450 × (15)^2 (1 mark)
= $\frac{1}{2}$ × 450 × 225 (1 mark)
= 50 625 J (1 mark)

This is another formula provided on the examination paper. A common error is to square the whole of the right-hand side of the equation, rather than just the speed. A mark has been allowed here for completing this part of the calculation correctly.

d efficiency = fraction of work transferred to where it is needed
= 50 625 ÷ 90 000 (1 mark)
= 0.56 (1 mark)

In this case the energy needed is the kinetic energy of the caravan. An answer of 56% would be allowed if efficiency was calculated as a percentage.

e It goes to heat in the tyres/road/surroundings (1 mark)

Unit 24

The Check Up

1 Three from: rocks, plants, the Sun, space, the Earth
2 Two from: medical uses, nuclear power, nuclear weapons
3 The nucleus **4** The radiation is random and varies
5 beta **6** alpha **7** alpha **8** beta **9** alpha **10** gamma **11** gamma
12 Gamma radiation is the only one that can penetrate the ground **13** The average time taken for the number of undecayed nuclei in a sample to halve **14** 2.5 g
15 The radiation cannot penetrate the air gap **16** It is the most intensely ionising and can cause most damage to cells
17 Geiger–Müller tube **18** All of the alpha radiation would be absorbed. Beta radiation is partially absorbed **19** $\frac{1}{16}$ **20** Moon rock does not contain any material that has been alive

Exam Practice

1 a i) 450 368 306 250 203 171 139 111 91 (1 mark)
ii) The emissions are random (1 mark)
Averaging over ten seconds gives a more reliable result (1 mark)

Always emphasise the random nature of radioactive decay when explaining why results may vary.

b i) The background radiation. (1 mark)
ii) Measure the background radiation over a certain time interval (e.g. 1 minute) and work out the average number of counts/s (1 mark)
Subtract this from each of the recorded counts/s (1 mark)

Background radiation is also random and can vary significantly over a one minute interval.

c i) Suitable choice of scale with correct labelling of each axis, including appropriate units (1 mark)
Correct plotting of all nine points (2 marks)
(allow one mark for up to three errors)
Smooth curve drawn (1 mark)

When drawing smooth curves on graphs, turn the paper so that you can use your arm like a compass, with your elbow as the pivot.

ii) For taking one reading of half-life from the graph, in the range 3.5–3.6 minutes (1 mark)
For taking a second reading in the same range (1 mark)

For working out the average value (1 mark)

When taking readings from graphs, always draw lines from the axes to the curve to show where you have taken the readings. Try to avoid using plotted points, take readings from the curve instead.

d i) The decay rate decreases with increasing time (1 mark)

Note how it is important to specify the change in both variables for the answer to be clear.

ii) As the polonium decays, there are fewer undecayed nuclei remaining (1 mark)

2 a *Radioactive*: the nucleus is unstable (1 mark)
It gives off radioactivity as it changes to a more stable form (1 mark)
Gamma radiation: is short-wavelength (1 mark) electromagnetic radiation (1 mark)

High frequency is an acceptable alternative for short-wavelength.

Half-life: is the average time taken (1 mark) for the number of undecayed nuclei to halve (1 mark)

b i) One from: Photographic film or a Geiger–Müller tube or a gamma camera (1 mark)
ii) Gamma radiation can penetrate the body tissue to be detected outside (1 mark)
iii) Alpha and beta radiation would be absorbed by body tissue (1 mark)
They could cause cell damage/cancer (1 mark)

An answer such as 'they could harm the patient' is too vague to be awarded any marks.

Notes

NOTES

This edition published exclusively for WHSmith, 2000, by:
Stanley Thornes (Publishers) Ltd
Ellenborough House
Wellington Street
CHELTENHAM GL50 1YW

00 01 02 03 04 / 10 9 8 7 6 5 4 3 2 1

A catalogue record for this book is available from the British Library.

ISBN 0-7487-5489-X

Designed by Rocket Design Ltd, London

Typeset by Oxford Designers & Illustrators

Printed and bound in Italy by G.Canale & C.S.p.A., Borgaro T.se, Turin